The All New TV Trivia Quiz Book

By the Same Authors

The TV Trivia Quiz Book
The TV Commercials Trivia Quiz Book
The Gossip Trivia Quiz Book
Dick Clark's The First 25 Years of Rock 'n' Roll
The Rock 'n' Roll Trivia Quiz Book
The Pow! Zap! Wham! Comic Book Trivia Quiz

The All New TV Trivia Quiz Book

Michael Uslan
and
Bruce Solomon

HARMONY BOOKS
New York

To Sarah Rose Uslan . . . welcome to a world full of Flubberdubs, Big Birds, Lassies, Lamb Chops, Bunny Rabbits, Flippers, Furys, and Pinky Lees.

Published by Harmony Books, a division of Crown Publishers, Inc., One Park Avenue, New York, New York 10016 and simultaneously in Canada by General Publishing Company Limited

HARMONY and colophon are trademarks of Crown Publishers, Inc.

Manufactured in the United States of America

Library of Congress Cataloging in Publication Data

Usland, Michael, 1951–
The all new TV trivia quiz book.

1. Television programs—United States—Miscellanea.
I. Solomon, Bruce. II. Title.
PN1992.9.U78 1985 791.45 85-7618
ISBN 0-517-55849-1 (pbk.)

Book design by Ron McCutchan

10 9 8 7 6 5 4 3 2 1
First Edition

Contents

Acknowledgments

Bruce and Michael want to thank the people who helped make this book possible: Pamela Gibbons and her flying fingers; Barry Milberg for his collection of photographs; Miles Laboratories, Inc., for the photo of Speedy Alka-Seltzer; Susan Breitner; the people who bought our first 12-inch Andrea—Ernie and Shirley Solomon; the people who bought our first 12-inch Crosley—Joe and Lil Uslan; and the fine folks we battled for control of the TV dial— Paul, Nancy, David, Sarah, Glen, Lisa, and Leah. Special thanks too to those who provided all the TV trivia material: Noel Neill, Jack Larson, Professor Pepperwinkle, Rupert Ritzig, Artemus Gordon, B. A. Barracas, B. J. Hunnicut, Officer Joe Bolton, Fireman Todd Russell, Millburn Drysdale, Pahoo Katawa, Gidney and Cloyd, El Exigente, Wilbur Hatch conducting the Desi Arnaz Orchestra, and, of course, Lassie.

The Joy of Sets

WARNING: There will be no questions concerning Clarence Clemons or Stradivarius in this book because we do not want to encourage more sax and violins on TV.

For the rest of the book, however, we will live by that old saying, "It is better to watch a single television show than to curse the darkness."

If, over the years, you tuned in a television set to watch *I Love Lucy, M*A*S*H, The Honeymooners,* or *60 Minutes,* then this book is for you. Whether you sat in the dark to watch *M Squad, I Spy,* or *The A-Team,* you can win a TV trivia letter for your sweater.

Trivia—those memories and facts buried deep in your psyche and always on the tip of your tongue. What was the name of the Italian mouse on *The Ed Sullivan Show*? What does "kimo sabe" mean? Would *you* like to be *Queen for a Day*?

This is no ordinary trivia book! *The All New TV Trivia Quiz Book* tests your wits against 1,001 new and improved trivia questions featuring your favorite TV characters from Jed Clampett and Robinson J. Peepers to J. R. Ewing and Alexis Carrington.

So turn on, tune in, and PLAY TRIVIA!!

Michael Uslan
Bruce Solomon
Chained to a TV set
somewhere in New Jersey,
1985

It's June 1955 and the Uslan/Solomon cousins line up to watch Ricky and Fred of *I Love Lucy* play a trick on Lucy and Ethel to teach them a lesson.

It's June 1985 and the Uslan/Solomon cousins (from top to bottom: Dr. Glen Solomon, Dr. Howard Solomon, Dr. Charles Hyman, Dr. Paul Hyman, Dr. Paul Uslan, Michael Uslan, Esq., and Bruce Solomon, Esq.) line up to watch Ricky and Fred play a trick on Lucy and Ethel to teach them a lesson on the 12,952nd rerun of *I Love Lucy*.

This is a Job for Superman!

Questions

Faster than a speeding bullet, answer these questions about the man of steel and his friends from The Adventures of Superman *for 1 point each.*

1. *FOR 3 TRIVIA POINTS* and to get you in the mood, recite the opening to *The Adventures of Superman.*

2. Who played Superman?

3. Two actresses portrayed Lois Lane. The first Lois was brash and tough and had a great scream. The second Lois was pert and friendly and had a million-dollar smile. Can you name both actresses?

4. Since *The Adventures of Superman* went off the air, this actor has written for the Metropolitan Opera and the Joffrey Ballet, and has become a Hollywood producer. But he first came to fame as Jimmy Olsen, the *Daily Planet*'s cub reporter. Who is he?

5. For 1 point each, who played irascible editor Perry White and Metropolis' top plainsclothes cop, Inspector Bill Henderson?

6. Can you name the absentminded professor, played by Phillip Tead in five episodes of the show, whose wacky inventions drove Superman crazy?

a. Uncle Oscar
b. Professor Twiddle
c. Professor Pepperwinkle
d. Professor Sterling Holloway
e. Horatio Hinkle

7. Which three of these inventions were *not* created by the good professor?

a. Antimemory vapor
b. Mr. McTavish, the Kryptonite-powered robot
c. Mr. Kelso, the mechanical mind
d. A machine that turned things topsy-turvy
e. A machine that let people travel by telephone
f. An antigravity formula
g. A time machine
h. A machine that turned platinum into gold

8. Which of the following villains was never on *The Adventures of Superman*?

a. Muscles McGurk
b. Legs Leemie
c. Muggsy Maples
d. Georgie Gleep
e. Slouchy McGoon
f. Clippy Jones
g. Leftover Louie Lyman
h. Cy Horton
i. Lex Luthor
j. Happy King
k. Lefty
l. Carny
m. Duke Taylor
n. Jake Morrell

9. In the "And Don't Call Me Chief" department, what did Perry White always yell when he got exasperated?

10. Metropolis was visited by a diminutive Martian, known on earth as Mr. Zero, who was banished from his home planet for being a quarter of an inch smaller than everybody else. What was Mr. Zero's official Martian name?

11. Where did Clark Kent go when he loosened his tie, took off his glasses, and turned into the Man of Steel?

12. In one episode, Superman was lured into a pit with Lois and Jimmy. While a Kryptonite ray zapped his strength, the walls of the pit started closing in. In what improbable way did they escape?

13. *The Adventures of Superman* was not well known for its extravagant special-effects budget. In the first two-part episode, "The Unknown People," what did the mole men use as a secret weapon?

14. For 1 point apiece, indicate with a yes or no whether each of the following was an actual episode of *The Adventures of Superman.*

a. Superman's uniform is stolen.__________
b. Superman gets amnesia.__________
c. Clark Kent sees a psychiatrist.__________
d. Red Kryptonite turns Superman evil.__________
e. Jimmy Olsen is given one million dollars.__________
f. Superman is frozen and loses his powers.__________
g. Superman marries Joi Lansing.__________
h. Superman splits in two.__________
i. Jimmy Olsen becomes editor of the *Daily Planet.*__________
j. Lois Lane is mistaken for the 2,026-year-old princess of Zaharan.__________
k. Superman turns back time to save Lois Lane.__________
l. Superman passes his molecules through a mysterious cube.__________
m. Chuck Connors plays Superman.__________
n. Jimmy Olsen is Prince Gregory of Burgonia.______
o. Jimmy Olsen's mother sells Folgers coffee on TV.__________
p. Jimmy Olsen impersonates Humphrey Bogart as a detective.__________
q. Perry White's sister is captured by a voodoo witch doctor.__________
r. Superman reveals his secret identity to Perry, Lois, and Jimmy. __________
s. Jimmy gets caught in a speed trap and the town disappears.__________

t. Superman gets help from Carmelita the brainy burro.__________

u. Lois disguises herself as a maid to beat Clark to a scoop.__________

v. Superman visits little Ricky's birthday party and saves Lucy. __________

w. Superman foils a criminal when a boy remembers an elephant registration number.__________

x. Thanks to positive Kryptonite, Lois and Jimmy get superpowers.__________

y. Superman goes to bed with Lois Lane and loses his powers.__________

15. *FOR 5 TRIVIA POINTS* What was the name of the apartment house Clark Kent lived in?

Answers

1. "Faster than a speeding bullet! More powerful than a locomotive! Able to leap tall buildings in a single bound! Look! Up in the sky! It's a bird! It's a plane! It's Superman!
"Yes, it's Superman—strange visitor from another planet who came to earth with powers and abilities far beyond those of mortal men. Superman—who could change the course of mighty rivers; bend steel in his bare hands! And who, disguised as Clark Kent, mild-mannered reporter for a great metropolitan newspaper, fights a never-ending battle for TRUTH, JUSTICE, AND THE AMERICAN WAY!"

2. George Reeves

3. Phyllis Coates was Lois Lane the first year and Noel Neill played the female reporter for the rest of the series.

4. Jack Larson

5. John Hamilton was in charge of the *Daily Planet* and Robert Shayne solved Metropolis' crimes . . . with a little help from the Man of Steel.

6. (c) Professor Pepperwinkle

7. (c) was created by Uncle Oscar, (f) was accidentally invented by Jimmy Olsen, and (g) was patented by Professor Twiddle. All the rest belonged to Professor Pepperwinkle.

8. (i) Superman's archvillain Lex Luthor was never on the TV show!

9. "Great Caesar's Ghost!"

10. Zero Zero Zero Minus One—"a real nothing"

11. The *Daily Planet*'s storeroom

12. Superman put Lois in a trance and levitated her. Her lacquered hair and high heels stopped the moving walls. Jimmy then shinned up the walls and turned the ray on the villains, giving Superman his power back.

13. A modified Electro-Lux vacuum cleaner

14. (a) yes, (b) yes, (c) yes, (d) no, (e) yes, (f) yes, (g) yes, (h) yes, (i) yes, (j) yes, (k) no, (l) yes, (m) yes, (n) yes, (o) no, (p) yes, (q) yes, (r) yes, (s) yes, (t) yes, (u) yes, (v) no, (w) yes, (x) yes, (y) no

15. The Standish Arms

Brought to You in Living Color

Questions

A color completes each of these TV titles. Fill in the correct answer for 1 point each.

16. *Hill Street _________s*

17. *Tenspeed and _________ Shoe*

18. *The _________ Shadow*

19. *The _________ Rose*

20. *Solid _________*

21. _________ *Lady and Jeff*

22. _________ *Spoons*

23. _________ *Thunder*

24. _________ *Ribbon Bouts*

25. *Boston _________ie*

26. *The __________ Skelton Show*

27. *Out of the __________*

28. *__________ Saddle*

29. *Bay City __________s*

30. *The __________ Buttons Show*

Answers

16. Blue
17. Brown
18. White
19. Yellow
20. Gold

21. Pink
22. Silver
23. Blue
24. Blue
25. Black

26. Red
27. Blue
28. Black
29. Blue
30. Red

Put You in Your Place

Answers

Match the TV show with its locale for 1 point each.

31. *Magnum, P.I.*	Boulder
32. *Dynasty*	Brooklyn
33. *Happy Days*	Washington, D.C.
34. *Barney Miller*	London
35. *Gunsmoke*	Virginia City
36. *Hotel*	Fernwood
37. *Mork and Mindy*	Hawaii
38. *The Bob Newhart Show*	Los Angeles
39. *Newhart*	Denver
40. *All in the Family*	Dallas
41. *Cheers*	Milwaukee
42. *The Bionic Woman*	Fort Baxter
43. *Welcome Back, Kotter*	Dodge City
44. *Lou Grant*	Clinton Corners
45. *Little House on the Prairie*	San Francisco
46. *The Waltons*	New Orleans

47.	*Bonanza*	New York City
48.	*Sgt. Bilko*	Queens
49.	*Mary Hartman, Mary Hartman*	Walnut Grove
50.	*Eight Is Enough*	Jefferson County
51.	*The Avengers*	Boston
52.	*Carter Country*	Chicago
53.	*The Farmer's Daughter*	Ojai
54.	*Bourbon Street Beat*	Sacramento
55.	*Dallas*	Vermont

Answers

31. Hawaii
32. Denver
33. Milwaukee
34. New York City
35. Dodge City
36. San Francisco
37. Boulder
38. Chicago
39. Vermont
40. Queens
41. Boston
42. Ojai
43. Brooklyn
44. Los Angeles
45. Walnut Grove
46. Jefferson County
47. Virginia City
48. Fort Baxter
49. Fernwood
50. Sacramento
51. London
52. Clinton Corners
53. Washington, D.C.
54. New Orleans
55. Dallas

Against the Law

Questions

The verdict is yours! Read these TV Guide*-type descriptions of famous lawyer shows and select the correct title from the following list for 1 point each. And remember . . . the decision of the judges is final!*

Adam's Rib
Petrocelli
The Defenders
Perry Mason
The New Adventures of Perry Mason
The People's Court
Owen Marshall, Counselor at Law
Kaz
Rosetti and Ryan
Arrest and Trial
The Law
The Lawyers (The Bold Ones)
Divorce Court
Traffic Court
The Young Lawyers
Night Court
Bachelor Father
The Storefront Lawyers
The Paper Chase
Judd for the Defense

56. Professor Kingsfield tells his students they'll get their grades the old-fashioned way—they'll earn them—while prize pupil Hart discusses the legal problems of moving a cancelled series to cable TV. ____________

57. While D.A. Ham Burger grills a witness, Della waits for Paul Drake to rush to the office with evidence that will finger the guilty party. ____________

58. Old man Carl bets that his high-priced Texas lawyer will jet into town to get him off. ____________

59. Murray Stone hails a taxi and wonders whether to practice law for the poor or win an Emmy for acting in a new TV series, *Judd Hirsch for the Defense*. ____________

60. The kindly senior partner instructs his associate, Jess Brandon, to get a six-million-dollar settlement in a personal injury suit. ____________

61. Judge Edgar Allen Jones Jr. offers the defendant a choice—$30 or 30 days for doing 45 in a 25 mph zone.

____

62. Judge Voltaire Perkins renders another decision on behalf of marital stability and higher ratings. ____________

63. Judge Harry Stone arraigns funny floozies while Bull the Bailiff looks menacing. ____________

64. An ex-con joins a prestigious L.A. law firm and works part time as a jazz drummer while viewers wonder how he passed the moral turpitude questions on the bar exam. ____________

65. Brian Darrell does the research and young Neil Darrell stretches the law to save a client while senior partner Walter Nichols sings "A Little Bitty Tear" and wonders why his obviously Italian associates have such WASPy names. ____________

66. Detective Sergeant Nick Anderson spends 45 minutes finding the perpetrator and within another 45 minutes attorney John Egan gets him off scot free.________

67. A Harvard Law School grad moves to San Remo in the Southwest, lives in a camper, and struggles to make ends meet in what is obviously a scriptwriter's fantasy.

____

68. David Hansen gives up a lucrative Century City practice to join Deborah Sullivan and Gabriel Kaye in a nonprofit establishment that provides legal services to the poor.________________________

69. *The Mod Squad* goes to law school as a street-smart black woman joins forces with a long-haired idealist and a wimpy yuppie to battle drug busts and slumlords in a neighborhood law office.____________________

70. Judge Joseph Wapner dispenses justice with common sense as he orders the bailiff to slice the baby in half.____________________

71. While his father, Lawrence, argues in court and takes Maalox tablets, Kenneth Preston hears the story of a lovely lady who was bringing up three very lovely girls.____________________

72. Brash, well-to-do Joe teams up with Frank, a former cop who got his law degree at night, but they lose on appeal to A. C. Nielsen.____________________

73. Assistant D.A. Bonner spars with his wife, Amanda, in the courtroom and in the bedroom.____________________

74. Hollywood lawyer Bentley Gregg avoids the incessant meddling of his niece, Kelly, and houseboy, Peter, long enough to go out on a date with Joan Collins.____________________

75. Monte Markham is unbeatable in court until he is haunted by the ghost of Raymond Burr.____________________

Answers

56. *The Paper Chase*
57. *Perry Mason*
58. *Judd for the Defense*
59. *The Law*
60. *Owen Marshall, Counselor at Law*
61. *Traffic Court*
62. *Divorce Court*
63. *Night Court*
64. *Kaz*
65. *The Lawyers (The Bold Ones)*
66. *Arrest and Trial*
67. *Petrocelli*
68. *The Storefront Lawyers*
69. *The Young Lawyers*
70. *The People's Court*
71. *The Defenders*
72. *Rosetti and Ryan*
73. *Adam's Rib*
74. *Bachelor Father*
75. *The New Adventures of Perry Mason*

Who's Who?

Questions

Identify the actor correctly after Clue A for 5 points, after Clue B for 3 points, or after Clue C for 1 point.

76.

A. By drinking Super Juice, I turned from Carter Nash, mild-mannered police chemist, into Captain Nice, mild-mannered superhero.
B. I am the imperious Dr. Craig on *St. Elsewhere.*
C. I ride by night and by day as the voice of the supercar Kitt on *Knight Rider*.
I am ______________________.

77.

A. On *Slattery's People*, my first regular role in a TV series, I played Frank Radcliff.
B. I was Tom and Rudy's father, Axel Jordache, in *Rich Man, Poor Man* and the skipper of a slave ship in *Roots*.
C. I spent ten years on the tube as Lou Grant.
My name is ______________________.

78.

A. I was Gordy Howard, the weatherman, on *The Mary Tyler Moore Show*.
B. I played James Evans, Florida's husband and J.J.'s father, on *Good Times*.
C. They called me Toby, but my name was Kunta Kinte in *Roots*.
I am ______________________________.

79.

A. When I starred as Lieutenant Anthony Kidd of the homicide squad in the 1949 ABC series *Stand By For Crime*, my real first name was Myron.
B. After hosting game shows such as *Who Pays, Majority Rules,* and *The Big Surprise*, I narrated the syndicated series *Biography*.
C. Since 1968, I have been the king of hard-hitting interviewers and investigative journalists on *60 Minutes*.
My name is ______________________.

80.

A. I did sketches and comedy blackouts with Jonathan Winters on his 1956 NBC series.
B. Art Fleming thanked me every day on *Jeopardy*.
C. I was the announcer on *Saturday Night Live*.
I am ______________________________.

Answers

76. William Daniels
77. Edward Asner
78. John Amos
79. Mike Wallace
80. Don Pardo

Odd and End Couples

Questions

For 1 trivia point each, answer these Odd Couple *questions correctly.*

81. On what month and day was Felix Unger asked by his wife to remove himself from his place of residence?

82. Oscar was a sportswriter for:
  a. The *New York Post*
  b. The *Daily News*
  c. The *New York Herald*
  d. The *New York Tribune*
  e. The *New York Journal-American*

83. What was Felix and Oscar's address on *The Odd Couple*?

84. Penny Marshall played Oscar's secretary, Myrna. What was her last name?

85. Name Felix's ex-wife.

86. Name Oscar's ex-wife.

87. Who are the six men found at the boys' regular poker game?

88. Who played Oscar and Felix in the movie version of *The Odd Couple*?

89. Who were the English sisters who lived above the boys?

90. What question does the narrator ask in the opening of each show?

Answers

81. November 13

82. (c) *The New York Herald*

83. 1049 Park Avenue, Apartment 1102, New York City

84. Turner

85. Gloria

86. Blanche

87. Oscar, Felix, Murray, Speed, Roy, and Vinnie

88. Walter Matthau and Jack Lemmon

89. Gwen and Cecily, the Pigeon sisters

90. "Can two divorced men share an apartment without driving each other crazy?"

Friendly Characters

Questions

Kids on TV series have always had good friends. We'll give you the name of the buddy and you identify whose friend he or she was for 1 point each. Choose from the following:

Dennis Mitchell (*Dennis the Menace*)
Jeff Miller (*Lassie*)
Jeff Stone (*The Donna Reed Show*)
Beaver Cleaver (*Leave It to Beaver*)
Wally Cleaver (*Leave It to Beaver*)
Bud Anderson (*Father Knows Best*)
Gidget Lawrence (*Gidget*)
Richie Petrie (*The Dick Van Dyke Show*)
Ricky Nelson (*The Adventures of Ozzie & Harriet*)

91. Tommy Anderson ______________________
92. Porky Brockway ______________________
93. Larry Mondello ______________________
94. Wally ______________________
95. Gilbert ______________________
96. Smitty ______________________
97. Joey MacDonald ______________________
98. Whitey Whitney ______________________
99. Larue ______________________

100. Kippy Watkins ______________________________
101. Eddie Haskell ______________________________
102. Lumpy Rutherford __________________________
103. Judy Hessler _______________________________
104. Margaret Wade _____________________________
105. Freddie Halper _____________________________

Answers

91. Dennis Mitchell
92. Jeff Miller
93. Beaver Cleaver
94. Ricky Nelson
95. Beaver Cleaver
96. Jeff Stone
97. Dennis Mitchell
98. Beaver Cleaver
99. Gidget Lawrence
100. Bud Anderson
101. Wally Cleaver
102. Wally Cleaver
103. Beaver Cleaver
104. Dennis Mitchell
105. Richie Petrie

And So On

Questions

Like bread and butter or Laurel and Hardy, certain things just belong together. We'll give you half the TV title and you complete it for 1 point.

106. *Cagney and . . .*
107. *Hardcastle and . . .*
108. *Simon and . . .*
109. *Kate and . . .*
110. *Scarecrow and . . .*
111. *Agronsky and . . .*
112. *Burns and . . .*
113. *Mork and . . .*
114. *The Young and . . .*
115. *Josie and . . .*
116. *Abbott and . . .*
117. *Amos 'n' . . .*
118. *Anna and . . .*
119. *Arrest and . . .*
120. *Arthur Godfrey and . . .*
121. *Calvin and . . .*
122. *The Captain and . . .*
123. *Captain Video and . . .*
124. *Feather and . . .*
125. *Harrigan and . . .*
126. *Hollywood and . . .*
127. *Holmes and . . .*
128. *Kukla, Fran, and . . .*
129. *Mr. T and . . .*
130. *My World and . . .*
131. *Pink Lady and . . .*
132. *Pistols 'n' . . .*
133. *Tenspeed and . . .*
134. *The Law and . . .*
135. *Stand Up and . . .*

Answers

106. *Lacey*
107. *McCormick*
108. *Simon*
109. *Allie*
110. *Mrs. King*
111. *Company*
112. *Allen*
113. *Mindy*
114. *the Restless*
115. *the Pussycats*
116. *Costello*
117. *Andy*
118. *the King*
119. *Trial*
120. *His Friends*
121. *the Colonel*
122. *Tennille*
123. *His Video Rangers*
124. *Father*
125. *Son*
126. *the Stars*
127. *YoYo*
128. *Ollie*
129. *Tina*
130. *Welcome to It*
131. *Jeff*
132. *Petticoats*
133. *Brown Shoe*
134. *Mr. Jones*
135. *Cheer*

Who Was that Masked Man?

Questions

Answer these questions about The Lone Ranger *for 1 point each. Hi-yo Silver, away!*

136. Who played the Lone Ranger's faithful Indian companion, Tonto?

137. Tonto always called the Lone Ranger "kimo sabe." What does "kimo sabe" mean?

a. White man with mask
b. Fearless warrior
c. Seeker of Justice
d. Faithful friend
e. Dogbreath

138. With his stature and distinctive voice, TV viewers knew that there was only one real Lone Ranger—Clayton Moore. But the producers once figured anybody could play a masked man and hired another actor to portray the Lone Ranger from 1952 to 1954. Can you name him?

BONUS—FOR 3 TRIVIA POINTS Name the actor who played the masked man in the ill-fated movie *The Legend of the Lone Ranger*.

139. What classical music was used as the stirring theme of *The Lone Ranger*?

140. We all know that the Lone Ranger rode the great white stallion Silver, but what was the name of Tonto's trusty steed?

a. Stainless Steel
b. Diablo
c. Tornado
d. Old Paint
e. Scout

141. When the masked man and Tonto headed off in different directions to track down the desperadoes, they always seemed to meet at the same place in every episode. Where was it?

a. By the twisted tree
b. At the old rock
c. By a stream at the outskirts of town
d. On the Santa Fe Trail
e. At the Stage Door Deli

142. The Lone Ranger had a trademark, something he always left with the people he helped. What was it?

143. An outlaw lured six Texas Rangers into an ambush, killing five and leaving the sixth for dead. What was the name of that sixth man who became the Lone Ranger?

BONUS—FOR 3 TRIVIA POINTS What was the name of the outlaw?

144. The Lone Ranger had a nephew who occasionally joined him on adventures during college vacations. What was his name?

BONUS—FOR 3 TRIVIA POINTS What was the name of his nephew's horse?

145. *FOR 5 TRIVIA POINTS* Recite the opening to *The Lone Ranger*.

Answers

136. Jay Silverheels

137. (d) Faithful friend

138. John Hart

BONUS—Klinton Spillsbury, a male model whose voice was dubbed in the film by James Keach

139. *The William Tell Overture* by Rossini

140. (e) Scout

141. (b) At the old rock

142. A silver bullet ("And I didn't get to thank him.")

143. John Reid

BONUS—Butch Cavendish

144. Dan Reid

BONUS—Victor

145. "A fiery horse with the speed of light, a cloud of dust, and a hearty 'Hi-yo Silver!'—the Lone Ranger. With his faithful Indian companion, Tonto, the daring and resourceful masked rider of the plains led the fight for law and order in the early West. Return with us now to those thrilling days of yesteryear. The Lone Ranger rides again!"

Say It Again, Sam!

Questions

Did you ever say something really clever and then hear people repeating your phrase? Well, it happens on TV all the time. One night a character delivers a deathless line and the next morning it is on millions of lips across America. Identify the show associated with the TV catchphrase for 1 point each.

146. "Hey, let's be careful out there."
147. "A-A-A-A-A-A-Y!"
148. "Book 'em, Dano!"
149. "Come on down!!!"
150. "Jeepers, Mr. Kent!"
151. "Hey, kids, what time is it?"
152. "Say the secret word and you'll divide an extra $100. It's a common word, something you see every day."
153. "Dy-no-mite!"
154. "Holy mackerel, Andy!"
155. "Na nu, na nu!"
156. "Do you want to go for the box or the curtain Carol Merrill is standing by?"
157. "I'd like you to meet my brother, George."

158. "You bet your bippy!"
159. "Hi-yo Silver, away!"
160. "You unlock this door with the key of imagination."
161. "It can't be done, Captain!"
162. "Sock it to me!"
163. "And that's the name of that tune!"
164. "Say goodnight, Gracie!"
165. "Goodnight, Chet . . . Goodnight, David!"

Answers

146. *Hill Street Blues*
147. *Happy Days*
148. *Hawaii Five-O*
149. *The Price Is Right*
150. *The Adventures of Superman*
151. *Howdy Doody*
152. *You Bet Your Life*
153. *Good Times*
154. *Amos 'n' Andy*
155. *Mork and Mindy*
156. *Let's Make a Deal*
157. *The Liberace Show*
158. *Rowan and Martin's Laugh-In*
159. *The Lone Ranger*
160. *The Twilight Zone*
161. *Star Trek*
162. *Rowan and Martin's Laugh-In*
163. *Baretta*
164. *The Burns and Allen Show*
165. *The Huntley-Brinkley Report*

Rock Around the Tube

Questions

From American Bandstand *to MTV, rock 'n' roll and television have grown up together. Crank your brain up to 45 rpm and score 1 point for each correct musical answer.*

166. Name the original five MTV video jocks.

167. One of the best TV movies ever made was *Elvis*. *FOR 2 TRIVIA POINTS EACH* Answer these questions about that flick.

a. Who gave an incredible performance as Elvis Presley?
b. Who played Elvis' sweetheart and wife, Priscilla Beaulieu Presley?
c. Who directed *Elvis* before coming to fame with *Halloween, The Fog, Escape From New York,* and *The Thing*?
d. What famous TV performer was the executive producer of *Elvis*?
e. When it was first shown, *Elvis* was pitted against two blockbuster movies during the February 1979 rating sweeps week. Can you name the two movies *Elvis* beat in becoming the top-rated show of that week?

168. Which teen heartthrob was the lead singer of TV's *The Partridge Family*?

a. Bobby Sherman
b. David Cassidy
c. Shaun Cassidy
d. Ted Cassidy
e. Hopalong Cassidy

169. Who has *not* been a host of the syndicated series *Solid Gold*?

a. Dionne Warwick
b. Marilyn McCoo
c. Andy Gibb
d. Rex Smith
e. Bubba Smith

170. Before he became a middle-of-the-road country star, this singer fronted a psychedelic rock group and hosted the syndicated variety series *Rollin' on the River*. Can you name him and his band?

171. True or False. Both the Beatles and Michael Jackson have been the stars of Saturday morning cartoon shows.

172. Don't doubt the power of TV to sell records. On November 15, 1954, a *Studio One* drama about the record industry featured a weepy ballad by an unknown singer. Within a week, the record sold 500,000 copies and eventually went beyond one million to become the Number One hit in America. It was the singer's only Top Forty record. *FOR 5 TRIVIA POINTS* Name the song (which was also the title of the show) and the singer.

173. Name the Monkees.

174. Who were the Blues Brothers?

175. Which of the following was *not* a regular feature of *American Bandstand*?

a. The autograph table
b. Rate-a-record
c. Spotlight dance
d. Go-go dancer in a cage
e. Asking dancers their names and ages
f. Top Ten countdown
g. Lip-synching by guest recording artists
h. Kids sitting in bleachers
i. Clearasil commercials

Answers

166. J. J. Jackson, Martha Quinn, Mark Goodman, Nina Blackwood, and Alan Hunter.
167. (a) Kurt Russell; (b) Season Hubley; (c) John Carpenter; (d) Dick Clark; (e) *Gone with the Wind* and *One Flew Over the Cuckoo's Nest*
168. (b) David Cassidy
169. (e) Bubba Smith
170. Kenny Rogers and the First Edition
171. True
172. "Let Me Go, Lover" by Joan Weber
173. Michael Nesmith, Peter Tork, Mickey Dolenz, and Davy Jones
174. Joliet Jake and Elwood Blues, a.k.a. Dan Ackroyd and the late John Belushi of *Saturday Night Live*
175. (d) Go-go dancer in a cage

What's My Line?

Questions

Match the character with his or her occupation for 1 point each.

176.	Colt Seavers	Riveter
177.	John McIntyre	Schoolteacher
178.	Bob Collins	Restaurant owner
179.	Raynor Sarnac	Actress
180.	Jack Tripper	Freelance photographer
181.	Bob Hartley	Stunt man
182.	José Jimenez	Reconnaissance pilot
183.	Chester A. Riley	Psychologist
184.	Ann Marie	Doctor
185.	Jaime Sommers	Bellhop

Answers

176. Stunt man
177. Doctor
178. Freelance photographer
179. Reconnaissance pilot
180. Restaurant owner
181. Psychologist
182. Bellhop
183. Riveter
184. Actress
185. Schoolteacher

Enter and Sign in Please

Questions

Award 5 trivia points if you correctly identify the person after Clue A, 3 trivia points after Clue B, or 1 trivia point after Clue C.

186.

A. I was Jim Sinclair, star of *Cowboy in Africa.*
B. I was Jason McCord in *Branded.*
C. I was Lucas McCain, hero of *The Rifleman.*
My name is ______________________.

187.

A. In *Leave It to Larry,* I was Larry.
B. I was Frank MacBride in *Switch.*
C. Oliver Wendell Douglas was my name in *Green Acres.*
My name is ______________________.

188.

A. In 1952, I read Tootsie Roll commercials as the staff announcer on *Paul Whiteman's TV Teen Club.*
B. I was host of *The Saturday Night Beechnut Show.*

C. Even though I was on *Live Wednesday* and had a *World of Talent,* I've been called the world's oldest teenager.
I am ________________________________.

189.

A. I was co-host of the ill-fated and ill-rated TV newsmagazine *Summer Sunday U.S.A.*
B. I co-hosted *Weekend* with Lloyd Dobyns.
C. I was the co-anchor on *NBC News Overnight.*
I am ________________________________.

190.

A. In our 1975 show *Ghost Busters,* we played Kong and Spencer.
B. In the early days of TV, one of us starred in *The Cavalcade of Stars* and had his own comedy show while the other starred in *Crunch and Des.*
C. We are best known as Sergeant Morgan O'Rourke and Corporal Randolph Agarn on *F Troop.*
Our names are __________________________.

Answers

186. Chuck Connors
187. Eddie Albert
188. Dick Clark
189. Linda Ellerbee
190. Forrest Tucker and Larry Storch

Test Patterns

Questions

This is a test of the Emergency Trivia System. For the next ten questions, we will be conducting a test. Score 1 point every time you get the right answer to a question. This is only a test.

191. Name Jack Benny's wife, valet, and announcer.

192. What longtime announcer did hundreds of commercials for Cracker Barrel Cheese and Velveeta on *Kraft Television Theater* and *The Kraft Music Hall*?

193. True or False. Jackie Gleason once hosted such a TV flop that the show was cancelled after one week and Gleason went on the air the next week to spend the whole half-hour apologizing to the audience.

194. Remember how all three networks jumped on the *Animal House* bandwagon in 1979 with shows about fraternity house hilarity and hi-jinx? ABC had *Delta House*; CBS gave us *Co-Ed Fever*; NBC dished up *Brothers and Sisters*. None lasted longer than four months. Which one was so bad that it was cancelled after its "special preview," never making it to its regular time slot?

195. Another program to be cancelled after its first appearance was the infamous *Laugh-In* ripoff *Turn-On*, which ran for one highly annoying night on February 5, 1969. *FOR 3 TRIVIA POINTS* Who was the guest host of that ill-fated show?

196. What are the names of the telephone operator and the little girl that Lily Tomlin portrayed on *Laugh-In*?

197. What "slices, dices, peels, and cores"?

a. Ginsu
b. Vegematic
c. Kitchen Magician
d. Armorcote II
e. Popeil's Pocket Fisherman

198. Name the three ghosts who haunted Cosmo Topper. *FOR 3 EXTRA TRIVIA POINTS* Who played them?

199. Bert Parks hosted the Miss America Pageant for 25 years, from 1955 through 1979, before he was rather unceremoniously booted out. His replacement lasted one year. Who was he?

200. Who on TV are known as Moose and Squirrel?

Answers

191. Mary Livingston was Jack's wife, Eddie "Rochester" Anderson was his valet, and Don Wilson was his announcer.

192. Ed Herlihy

193. True. The disaster was called *You're in the Picture.*

194. *Co-Ed Fever*

195. Tim Conway

196. Ernestine was the operator and Edith Ann was the little girl.

197. (b) Vegematic

198. Marion Kirby ("The Ghostess with the Mostest") was played by Anne Jeffreys; George Kirby ("That Most Sporting Spirit"), was portrayed by Robert Sterling; and Neil, the drunken St. Bernard, was played by Buck.

199. Ron Ely, who used to be a bit of a swinger as TV's *Tarzan* in the late 1960s.

200. No, they're not the latest pair of prime-time cops. They're Rocky and Bullwinkle, otherwise known as Rocket J. Squirrel and Bullwinkle the Moose.

We'll Be Back After a Word From Our Sponsor

Questions

Could we forget the most important thing on TV . . . the commercials? Of course not! Now show how much you know about TV's favorite 30- and 60-second art form by identifying each product for 1 point apiece.

201. "It takes a licking, but keeps on ticking!" ______

202. "I can't believe I ate the whole thing!" ______

203. "My baloney has a first name!" ______

204. "Nothing says lovin' like something from the oven!" ______

205. "So flexible you can pick up a dime!" ______

206. "Lifts and separates!" ______

207. "A little dab'll do ya!" ______

208. "If you've got the time, we've got the beer!" ______

209. "Tan, don't burn!" ______

210. "Reach out and touch someone!" ______

211. "You can pay me now or pay me later!"________
212. "Two seconds gives you 24-hour protection!"______

____

213. "It's what's up front that counts!"____________
214. "99 and 44⁄100 percent pure!"_______________
215. "My wife . . . I think I'll keep her!"____________

BONUS—FOR 3 TRIVIA POINTS What kind of kids eat Armour hot dogs?____________________

Don't Let
ACID
INDIGESTION
chase away
your fun!
SPEEDY

(courtesy of Miles Laboratories, Inc.)

Answers

201. Timex watches
202. Alka-Seltzer
203. Oscar Meyer
204. Pillsbury
205. Playtex Living Gloves
206. Playtex Living Bra
207. Brylcreem
208. Miller beer
209. Coppertone
210. AT&T (Bell Telephone)
211. Fram Oil Filters
212. Right Guard deodorant
213. Winston cigarettes
214. Ivory soap
215. Geritol
BONUS. Fat kids, skinny kids, kids that climb on rocks. Tough kids, sissy kids, even kids with chicken pox.

I Got Them Old Hill Street Blues Again, Mama

Questions

Roll call 6:58 A.M. There are ten trivia questions posing problems on Hill Street, all claiming to be worth 1 point each. Get the collar on all ten, but be careful out there!

216. Until he succumbed to cancer in 1984, Michael Conrad conducted the roll call at the Hill Street station on every episode. What was the name of his character?

217. Pair up the Hill Street partners:

a.	Lucy Bates	Bobby Hill
b.	Andy Renko	Johnny LaRue
c.	Neil Washington	Joe Coffee

218. Who is the straitlaced, gun-loving leader of Hill Street's S.W.A.T. team?

219. What does Captain Furillo's main squeeze, Joyce Davenport, do for a living?

220. What is Joyce's term of endearment for Frank?

a. Squirrelhead
b. Dogbreath
c. Munchkin
d. Pizzaman
e. Everready

221. In one of LaRue's many money-making schemes, he became the manager of a stand-up comic. LaRue thought the comic's name was a problem and made a minor change, but the comic's real problem was narcolepsy. What was the name of this sleepy comedian?

222. Who is the undercover cop who growls, occasionally bites criminals, and is always called at work by his mother?

223. Who is Frank Furillo's boss?

224. Frank has two lieutenants working for him. One is a Hispanic who is worried about being passed over for promotion; the other is a soft-spoken hostage negotiator who had an affair with Frank's ex-wife. Can you name Furillo's right-hand men?

225. Which of the following were story lines on *Hill Street Blues*?

a. A costumed "superhero" fights crime on Hill Street.
b. A horse thief claims to be the Cisco Kid.
c. Frank Jr. runs away from home and Fay is frantic.
d. Esterhaus is torn between sexual gold medalist Grace Gardner and his fiancée who just graduated from high school.
e. Howard tries to commit suicide (but *TV Guide* spills the beans).
f. Renko is busted down to meter maid.
g. Bobby Hill has a boil on his butt.
h. Furillo shaves his head and asks Joyce, "Who loves ya, baby?"

Answers

216. Sergeant Phil Esterhaus
217. (a) Joe Coffee, (b) Bobby Hill, (c) Johnny LaRue
218. Lt. Howard Hunter
219. She was a public defender, but became an assistant DA during the 1984–1985 season
220. (d) Pizzaman
221. Vic Hitler, a name LaRue changed to Vic Hitler, Jr.
222. Mick Belker
223. Chief Fletcher Daniels
224. Ray Calletano and Henry Goldblume
225. All except (h)

Horse Sense

Questions

Match the cowboy to the horse for 1 trivia point each.

226.	The Lone Ranger	Topper
227.	Tonto	Silver
228.	Roy Rogers	Champion
229.	Dale Evans	Trigger
230.	The Cisco Kid	Tornado
231.	Pancho	Buttercup
232.	Hopalong Cassidy	Scout
233.	Gene Autry	Loco
234.	Zorro	Diablo
235.	Annie Oakley	Buttermilk

Answers

226. Silver
227. Scout
228. Trigger
229. Buttermilk
230. Diablo
231. Loco
232. Topper
233. Champion
234. Tornado
235. Buttercup

I'm Gonna Sit Right Down and Write Myself a Letter

Questions

Our initial premise here is that many TV shows have letters in their titles. Score 1 point for every letter-perfect answer. If you get them all right, give yourself an A+.

236. *The*____*–Team*
237. ____ *Squad*
238. ____ *Spy*
239. *Mayberry* ____.____.____.
240. ____.____. *Hooker*
241. ____.____.____. *Sharkey*
242. ____.____. *Crackerby*
243. *Hawaii Five-* ____
244. *Gomer Pyle* ____.____.____.____.
245. *The Man from* ____.____.____.____.____.
246. ____ ____ ____ ____ *in Cincinnati*
247. ____*____*____*____
248. ____.____.____.____. (East Coast cop show)
249. ____.____.____.____. (West Coast cop show)
250. *Magnum* ____.____.

251. ___ *Troop*
252. ___.___. *and the Bear*
253. *Mr.* ___ *and Tina*
254. *The* ___.___.___.
255. ___.___. *College Bowl*
256. *Elizabeth* ___
257. ___.___. *VII*
258. ___ ___ ___ *Stage 67*
259. *Harper Valley* ___.___.___.
260. *The Governor and* ___.___.
261. *Harry-*___
262. ___.___.___. *Cat*
263. ___.___.___. *Cats*
264. *Code* ___
265. *Marcus Welby,* ___.___.
266. *Match Game* ___.___.
267. *Quincy,* ___.___.
268. *The* ___.___.
269. ___ ___ ___ ___ (comedy)
270. *The* ___.___. *Steel Hour*
271. *Palmerstown,* ___.___.___.
272. ___.___.___. *Hudson Street*
273. *Trapper John,* ___.___.
274. *Malibu* ___
275. *Project* ___.___.___.

Answers

236. A
237. M
238. I
239. R.F.D.
240. T.J.
241. C.P.O.
242. O.K.
243. O
244. U.S.M.C.
245. U.N.C.L.E.
246. WKRP
247. M*A*S*H
248. N.Y.P.D.
249. S.W.A.T.
250. P.I.
251. F
252. B.J.
253. T
254. F.B.I.
255. G.E.
256. R
257. Q.B.
258. ABC
259. P.T.A.
260. J.J.
261. O
262. T.H.E.
263. B.A.D.
264. R
265. M.D.
266. P.M.
267. M.E.
268. D.A.
269. SCTV
270. U.S.
271. U.S.A.
272. A.E.S.
273. M.D.
274. U
275. U.F.O.

All the News that Fits, We Print

Questions

We interrupt this quiz for a special bulletin: "Trivia buff scores 1 point for each correct answer about the TV news! Film at eleven." We now return to your regularly scheduled quiz!

276. The original host of ABC News' *Nightline* was:

a. Howdy Doody
b. Alfred E. Newman
c. Ted Koppel
d. Tom Jarriel
e. Sam Donaldson

277. What incident inspired ABC to create *Nightline*?

278. When did NBC first team up Chet Huntley and David Brinkley?

279. Who was the anchorman for *Camel News Caravan* on NBC?

280. Who were the original three anchormen of ABC's *World News Tonight* and from what cities did they normally report?

281. Who was the anchorman of ABC's early evening newscast from 1953 through 1960?

a. Douglas Edwards
b. John Cameron Swayze
c. John Daly
d. Bud Collier
e. J. Fred Muggs

282. Whose slogan was "Give us 18 minutes and we'll give you the world"?

a. Satellite News Channel
b. Cable News Network
c. ABC News Brief
d. Independent Network News
e. The Playboy Channel

283. The co-anchors of ABC's early morning newscast, *World News This Morning*, are:

a. Bill Curtis and Diane Sawyer
b. John Palmer and Connie Chung
c. David Hartman and Joan Lunden
d. Steven Bell and Kathleen Sullivan
e. Randy Hundley and Christie Brinkley

284. Former anchorman Howard K. Smith has a son who is a correspondent for ABC News. His name is:

a. John Smith
b. Jack Smith
c. Howard K. Smith Jr.
d. Buffalo Bob Smith
e. Knucklehead Smith

285. True or False. Chris Wallace of NBC News is the son of *60 Minutes*' Mike Wallace.

286. When NASA launched the Mercury, Gemini, and Apollo space missions, who anchored the telecasts for ABC?

287. Before the days of Andy Rooney, *60 Minutes* had a segment called "Point—Counterpoint," featuring a lively debate from the liberal and conservative sides on an issue. Name the conservative spokesman and the two liberals he did battle with over the years.

288. Identify the network associated with all of the following newscasters: Roger Mudd, Connie Chung, Garrick Utley, Jessica Savitch, Linda Ellerbee, Frank McGee, and Irving R. Levine.

289. The weatherman on *The Today Show* is:

a. Willard Scott
b. Millard Fillmore
c. John Coleman
d. Bryant Gumbel
e. Lloyd Lindsey Young

290. Which of the following was not an NBC newsmagazine program?

a. *First Camera*
b. *First Tuesday*
c. *Prime Time Saturday*
d. *Prime Time Sunday*
e. *Summer Sunday U.S.A.*
f. *Weekend*
g. *Lost Weekend*
h. *Chronolog*
i. *NBC Magazine with David Brinkley*

291. In 1983, ABC tried a late night interview program called *One on One*. The host was:

a. Julius Erving
b. Greg Jackson
c. Keith Jackson
d. Reggie Jackson
e. Tom Snyder

292. To go along with *Today* and *Tonight*, NBC came up with a late night interview show called *Tomorrow*, starring Tom Snyder. When there was no more hope for *Tomorrow* in 1981, what show replaced it in the NBC late night lineup?

293. What newsman is famous for his *On the Road* reports?

a. Hughes Rudd
b. Bill Moyers
c. Charles Kuralt
d. Charles Osgood
e. Roger Miller

294. True or False. Peter Jennings was named anchorman for *The ABC Evening News* in 1965.

295. *FOR 10 TRIVIA POINTS* Here's a question for true trivia buffs. In 1967, an AFTRA strike forced Walter Cronkite off the air for two weeks. Name the bespectacled CBS lawyer who anchored *The CBS Evening News* in Cronkite's place and achieved short-lived notoriety.

Answers

276. (c) Ted Koppel
277. The Iranian hostage crisis
278. During the political conventions in 1956. They first co-anchored the news for NBC in October 1956.
279. John Cameron Swayze
280. Frank Reynolds in Washington, Max Robinson in Chicago, and Peter Jennings in London
281. (c) John Daly, who was also the host of *What's My Line?* on CBS
282. (a) Satellite News Channel
283. (d) Bell and Sullivan
284. (b) Jack Smith
285. True
286. ABC science editor Jules Bergman
287. Conservative James J. Kilpatrick sparred with liberals Nicholas Von Hoffman (1971–1974) and Shana Alexander (1975–1979).
288. NBC
289. (a) Willard Scott
290. (g) *Lost Weekend*
291. (b) Greg Jackson
292. *Late Night with David Letterman*
293. (c) Charles Kuralt
294. True. Jennings anchored ABC's newscast from 1965 to 1968, then resurfaced in 1978 on *World News Tonight* before becoming the sole anchor in 1983.
295. Arnold Zenker

Char-Actors

Questions

We'll give you the names of three TV characters. For 1 point each, tell us which actor played all three.

296. ________________ Pete Ryan, Alexander Mundy, Jonathan Hart

297. ________________ Murray Stone, Dominick Delvecchio, Alex Rieger

298. ________________ Conrad Siegfried, Jerry Bauman, Dr. Adam Bricker

299. ________________ Jim Street, Peter Campbell, Dan Tanna

300. ________________ Michael Endicott, Bentley Gregg, Blake Carrington

301. ________________ Heath Barkley, Steve Austin, Colt Seavers

302. ________________ R. B. Kingston, Robert Ironside, Perry Mason

303. ________________ Albert Miller, Tony Nelson, J. R. Ewing

304. ________________ Bill Davis, Dr. Sean Jamison, Judge Milton C. Hardcastle

305. ________________ Mr. Morrison, Ralph Furley, Barney Fife

306. ________________ Mike Hammer, Grey Holden, Carl Kolchak

307. ________________ Hoby Gilman, Bill Maxwell, Kelly Robinson

308. ____________________ George Russel, Jed Clampett, Barnaby Jones

309. ____________________ Will Chandler, Michael Alden, Detective Johnny Corso

310. ____________________ Senator Eugene Smith, Daniel Boone, Davy Crockett

Answers

296. Robert Wagner
297. Judd Hirsch
298. Bernie Kopell
299. Robert Urich
300. John Forsythe
301. Lee Majors
302. Raymond Burr
303. Larry Hagman
304. Brian Keith
305. Don Knotts
306. Darren McGavin
307. Robert Culp
308. Buddy Ebsen
309. Frank Converse
310. Fess Parker

Themes to Me I've Heard that Song Before

Questions

We'll tell you about a famous TV theme song and you name each show for 5 points.

311. There was a scout troop short a child while Khrushchev was due at Idlewild.

312. One day while a hunter was shooting at some food, up through the ground came a bubblin' crude.

313. He told his wife she could keep Manhattan; just give him that countryside.

314. People yakety-yak a streak and waste the time of day, but the star of this show would never talk unless he had something to say.

315. These cousins laughed alike, walked alike, and at times they would even talk alike.

316. From West Virginny this family came to stay in sunny Californ-i-a.

317. Uncle Joe was always moving kind of slow.

318. This theme asked you how your sense of humor was because there was a rumor that laughter was on its way.

319. The song for this show told us that when the West was very young there lived a man named . . .

320. When it was time to start this show, the cry went up to the kids, "Let's go!"

Answers

311. *Car 54, Where Are You?*
312. *The Beverly Hillbillies*
313. *Green Acres*
314. *Mr. Ed*
315. *The Patty Duke Show*
316. *The Real McCoys*
317. *Petticoat Junction*
318. *Candid Camera*
319. *Bat Masterson*
320. *Howdy Doody*

The Honeymooner's Over

Questions

Each correct answer about the TV classic The Honeymooners *is worth 2 points.*

321. Did the Kramdens or the Nortons live downstairs?

322. What was the name of the bus company that Ralph worked for?

323. Ralph's boss, the president of the bus company, was:

a. Mr. Manicotti
b. Mr. Monahan
c. Mr. McGillicutty
d. Mr. Lescoulie
e. June Taylor

324. Ralph and Ed belonged to:

a. The Loyal Order of the Water Buffalo
b. The Raccoon Lodge
c. The Henry Cabot Lodge
d. The Mystic Knights of the Sea
e. The Brotherhood of Temple Beth Howland

325. Alice Kramden's maiden name was:

a. DeFazio
b. Meadows
c. Norton
d. Gibson
e. Fink

326. When the boys were learning how to play golf from a book, Ralph instructed Ed to approach the tee and address the ball. What did Ed say?

327. Ralph went on a quiz show to strike it rich. During the practice sessions, he knew the composer of every song, except the one Ed played on the piano to introduce each selection. What was that song (which, of course, was the one Ralph was asked about on the show)?

328. Who was Morris Fink?

329. Name Ed's wife and the actress who originally played the role.

330. Music for *The Honeymooners* was produced and arranged by orchestra leader:
- a. Ray Bloch
- b. David Rose
- c. Skitch Henderson
- d. Sammy Spear
- e. Les Brown

331. What was the Kramdens' Brooklyn address?
- a. 328 Chauncey Street
- b. 704 Houser Street
- c. 1164 Morning Glory Circle
- d. 1313 Mockingbird Lane
- e. 485 Bonnie Meadow Road

332. When he was mad, Ralph threatened that one of these days he would send Alice (POW!) to the moon. But when he was making up, what did Ralph always say to her?

333. Who originated the role of Alice Kramden back in 1951?

334. From 1966 to 1970, who replaced Audrey Meadows as the long-suffering Alice Kramden?

335. *FOR 5 TRIVIA POINTS* Name the show on which *The Honeymooners* first regularly appeared as a skit.

Answers

321. The Kramdens
322. The Gotham Bus Company
323. (b) Mr. Monahan
324. (b) The Raccoon Lodge
325. (d) Gibson
326. "Hello, ball!"
327. "Swanee River"
328. The Grand Exalted High Ruler of the Raccoon Lodge
329. Trixie, played by Joyce Randolph
330. Both (a) Ray Bloch and (d) Sammy Spear provided the music over the years.
331. (a) 328 Chauncey Street
332. "Baby, you're the greatest!"
333. Pert Kelton
334. Sheila MacRae
335. *The Cavalcade of Stars*

Cartoon Quotient

Questions

Give yourself 1 point for each correct answer to these TV cartoon questions.

Name the cartoon character who was a native of:

336. Bedrock ______________________

337. Frostbite Falls, Minnesota ______________________

338. Galahad Glen ______________________

339. Jellystone Park ______________________

Match the cartoon hero to his loyal, true-blue sidekick:

340. Yogi Bear	Sherman
341. Quick Draw McGraw	Blabber Mouse
342. Mr. Peabody	Boo Boo
343. Crusader Rabbit	Hardy Har Har
344. Rocket J. Squirrel	Minute Mouse
345. King Leonardo	Baba Louie
346. Courageous Cat	Bullwinkle
347. Snooper	Dum Dum
348. Touché Turtle	Odie O. Colognie
349. Lippy the Lion	Rags the Tiger

350. Who is the friendliest ghost you know?

351. Fill in the blank. "Felix the Cat. The wonderful, wonderful cat. Whenever he gets in a fix, he reaches into his ______________________."

For 2 trivia points each, which cartoon character said:

352. "Sufferin' Succotash!" ____________________

353. "Yabba Dabba Doo!" ____________________

354. "I tawt I taw a puddy tat!" ____________________

355. "Exit—stage left!" ____________________

356. "That's a joke, son!" ____________________

357. "Never underestimate the power of a schnook!" ____________________

358. "Th–th–that's all folks!" ____________________

359. "Whoa, Nellie!" ____________________

360. "Hewo. Heh-heh-heh-heh-heh." ____________________

361. "What's up, doc?" ____________________

362. Name Popeye's four nephews.

363. Name Donald Duck's three nephews.

364. Name Mickey Mouse's two nephews.

365. Name Mr. Magoo's nephew.

366. The only male ever to get close to Betty Boop was her pet dog named:

a. Pluto
b. Bluto
c. Bimbo
d. Harlot
e. Koko

367. What was the name of Warner Brothers' romantic French-speaking skunk?

Match the villain to the cartoon hero for 1 trivia point each:

368. Oil Can Harry	Ruff and Ready
369. Dishonest John	Top Cat
370. Snidely Whiplash	Dick Tracy
371. Bluto	King Leonardo
372. Black Pete	Deputy Dawg
373. Dick Dastardly	Woody Woodpecker
374. The Munimula Men	Underdog
375. Boris Badenov and Natasha Fatale	The Pink Panther
376. The Inspector	Pixie and Dixie
377. The Fox	Herman
378. Mr. Jinx	Felix the Cat
379. Katnip	Baby Huey
380. Wally Walrus	Penelope Pitstop
381. The Professor	Popeye
382. Simon Bar Sinister	Rocky and Bullwinkle
383. Muskie	Mickey Mouse
384. Officer Dibble	Dudley Do-Right
385. Biggy Rat and Itchy Brother	Beanie and Cecil
386. Pruneface and Itchy	Mighty Mouse

387. *Identify this cartoon favorite after Clue A for 5 trivia points, after Clue B for 3 trivia points, or after Clue C for 1 trivia point.*

A. My name came from a spiritual leader of India.
B. My nemesis was Sourpuss.
C. I'm a Terrytoon character.
My name is ______________________.

388. Who was Tom Terrific's canine companion?

389. Where does Magilla Gorilla reside?
a. The Oval Office
b. The Peter Potamus Pet Emporium
c. Bongo Congo
d. Anywhere he wants to
e. Mr. Peebles' Pet Shop

390. What is the name of Dudley Do-Right's horse? (HINT: It wasn't Nell . . . that was his sweet girlfriend. It wasn't Inspector Fenwick . . . that was his boss.)

Answers

336. Fred Flintstone
337. Bullwinkle
338. Crusader Rabbit
339. Yogi Bear
340. Boo Boo
341. Baba Louie
342. Sherman
343. Rags the Tiger
344. Bullwinkle
345. Odie O. Cologne
346. Minute Mouse
347. Blabber Mouse
348. Dum Dum
349. Hardy Har Har
350. Casper
351. Bag of tricks
352. Sylvester
353. Fred Flintstone
354. Tweety
355. Snagglepuss
356. Foghorn Leghorn
357. Boris Badenov
358. Porky Pig
359. Quick Draw McGraw
360. Elmer Fudd
361. Bugs Bunny
362. Pipeye, Poopeye, Peepeye, and Pupeye
363. Huey, Dewey, and Louie
364. Morty and Ferdy
365. Waldo
366. (c) Bimbo
367. Pepe LePew
368. Mighty Mouse
369. Beanie and Cecil
370. Dudley Do-Right
371. Popeye
372. Mickey Mouse
373. Penelope Pitstop
374. Ruff and Ready
375. Rocky and Bullwinkle
376. The Pink Panther
377. Baby Huey
378. Pixie and Dixie
379. Herman
380. Woody Woodpecker
381. Felix the Cat
382. Underdog
383. Deputy Dawg
384. Top Cat
385. King Leonardo
386. Dick Tracy
387. Gandy Goose (or is it Gandhi Ghoose?)
388. The Mighty Manfred
389. (e) Mr. Peebles' Pet Shop
390. Horse

Home Maid

Questions

Maids, butlers, and houseboys have always been important to TV shows. Match the servant to the family he or she served for 1 point each.

391.	Hazel	Tate
392.	Louise	Davis
393.	Peter	Wayne
394.	French	Findlay
395.	Alfred	Jefferson
396.	Florida	Reid
397.	Florence	Gregg
398.	Kato	Addams
399.	Benson	Baxter
400.	Lurch	Williams

Answers

391. Baxter
392. Williams
393. Gregg
394. Davis
395. Wayne
396. Findlay
397. Jefferson
398. Reid
399. Tate
400. Addams

A Really Big Shew!

Questions

His variety show started in the summer of 1948, and for the next 23 years Ed Sullivan was a fixture on Sunday nights. The program featured virtually every major star as well as dramatic readings, ballet, dancing bears, and rock 'n' roll. Correct answers on the Great Stoneface score 1 point apiece.

401. What was the original title of *The Ed Sullivan Show*?

a. *Broadway Open House*
b. *Toast of the Town*
c. *You're the Top*
d. *The Big Event*
e. *King Sullivan's Mine*

402. Before he came to fame as host of a variety show, what was Ed Sullivan's occupation?

a. Newspaper columnist
b. Talent agent
c. Broadway producer
d. Sportscaster
e. Diction coach

403. At the time *The Ed Sullivan Show* went off the air in 1971, where was the show broadcast from every week?

404. True or False. When Elvis Presley first appeared on Ed's show on September 9, 1956, he was shown only from the waist up.

405. What was the name of the mechanical Italian mouse that frequented *The Ed Sullivan Show*?

406. Ed Sullivan's favorite ventriloquist was a man who used a made-up hand instead of a dummy and had a talking box that answered " 'S-all right!" What was his name?

407. Remember the man who spun dishes on upended poles to a certain piece of stirring music? What was that music?

a. "I Fall to Pieces"
b. *The 1812 Overture*
c. *Ride of the Valkyries*
d. *Sabre Dance*
e. "Stars and Stripes Forever"

408. Another of Ed's favorites was the Canadian comedy team of:

a. Rowan and Martin
b. Martin and Lewis
c. Grayson and Wayne
d. Wayne and Shuster
e. Simon and Schuster

409. What Broadway show featured the "Ode to Ed Sullivan" production number?

a. *Hair*
b. *Grease*
c. *Bye Bye Birdie*
d. *A Chorus Line*
e. *West Side Story*

410. When CBS cancelled *The Ed Sullivan Show* in 1971, what program replaced it in the Sunday night lineup?

Answers

401. (b) *Toast of the Town*
402. (a) Newspaper columnist
403. The Ed Sullivan Theater in New York
404. False. The infamous "from the waist up" telecast was actually Elvis' third Sullivan appearance, on January 6, 1957.
405. Topo Gigio
406. Señor Wences
407. (d) *Sabre Dance*
408. (d) Wayne and Shuster
409. (c) *Bye Bye Birdie*
410. *The CBS Sunday Night Movie*

TV Movies

Questions

Which of these TV series were based on motion pictures? Answer yes or no for 1 point each.

411. *Casablanca* ________
412. *M*A*S*H* ________
413. *Fame* ________
414. *Blue Thunder* ________
415. *Twilight Zone* ________
416. *Star Trek* ________
417. *Mr. Ed* ________
418. *Hogan's Heroes* ________
419. *Twelve O'Clock High* ________
420. *Gidget* ________
421. *Sheena* ________
422. *The Ghost and Mrs. Muir* ________
423. *Topper* ________
424. *The Thin Man* ________
425. *Daktari* ________
426. *Born Free* ________
427. *Please Don't Eat the Daisies* ________
428. *Perry Mason* ________
429. *The Courtship of Eddie's Father* ________
430. *The Virginian* ________
431. *The Big Valley* ________
432. *Mr. Roberts* ________
433. *Paper Moon* ________
434. *Lassie* ________
435. *Alice* ________

Answers

411. Yes
412. Yes
413. Yes
414. Yes
415. No
416. No
417. No
418. Yes. It was derived (very loosely) from *Stalag 17.*
419. Yes
420. Yes
421. No
422. Yes
423. Yes
424. Yes
425. Yes
426. Yes
427. Yes
428. No
429. Yes
430. Yes
431. No
432. Yes
433. Yes
434. Yes
435. Yes. It was based on *Alice Doesn't Live Here Anymore.*

Crossed Channels

Questions

Here's a tubeful of questions that jump around the screen from one subject to another. Each correct answer is worth 1 trivia point.

436. Forget Hollywood! Who cares about London or Paris? What interesting things ever happened in New York? Let's go to where the real action is. Have you ever heard of Cedar Grove, New Jersey? Well, then: True or False. ABC once had a prime-time network show called *Music from Cedar Grove.*

437. Which *Squad* shows never existed?

a. *Police Squad*
b. *Felony Squad*
c. *M Squad*
d. *Mod Squad*
e. *Bod Squad*
f. *Racket Squad*
g. *Squad Thrusts*
h. *Squad in the Woods*

438. Which of these was not a "jiggle" show?

a. *Charlie's Angels*
b. *Three's Company*
c. *We Got It Made*
d. *Mr. T and A-Team*

439. Sandy, the dizzy, gossipy neighbor in *Good Morning, World*, was played by:

a. Meryl Streep
b. Goldie Hawn
c. Jane Fonda
d. Sally Field
e. Katharine Hepburn

440. When *Fernwood 2-Night* became big time as *America 2-Night*, Barth Gimble moved the show to "the unfinished furniture capital of the world." *FOR 2 TRIVIA POINTS* Name this metropolis.

441. True or False. Marvin Hamlisch wrote the *Good Morning, America* theme.

442. True or False. Leonard Bernstein wrote *The Munsters* theme.

443. Which TV series starred Charles Bronson?

a. *Then Came Bronson*
b. *Bronk*
c. *Man with a Camera*
d. *Garrison's Gorillas*
e. *Bronco*

444. Who lived at 607 South Maple Street, Springfield?

445. Wo Fat was the archenemy of:

a. Richard Simmons
b. Batman
c. Steve McGarrett (*Hawaii Five-O*)
d. Captain Midnight
e. Hazel Burke

Answers

436. True
437. (e) *Bod Squad*, (g) *Squad Thrusts*, (h) *Squad in the Woods*
438. (d) *Mr. T and A-Team*
439. (b) Goldie Hawn
440. Alta Coma, California
441. True
442. False
443. (c) *Man with a Camera*
444. The Andersons on *Father Knows Best*
445. (c) Steve McGarrett (*Hawaii Five-O*)

Trivia Quiz Masters

Questions

Read these quizzical clues of famous quiz shows and identify the show for 1 point each.

446. "Contestants who say the secret word divide $100." ____________

447. Celebrity guest William Shatner shoots host Dick Clark when he sees that he must list "Things you don't find in your oven." ____________

448. The panel's blindfolds are all in place as the mystery guest enters and signs in please. ____________

449. "It's time for the 'Lightning Round.' Here's the first word. Go!" ____________

450. "You and Contestant Number Three are going to Hawaii with your chaperone!" ____________

451. "A recap shows John in the lead with $220, followed by Mary with $90. Betty, with minus $10, hasn't really started playing yet." ____________

452. "Unlike the other contestant, whose husband died the day after she was married, my husband died on our wedding night and, better still, our home and belongings were all repossessed." ______________

453. "Will the real Murray Finsterwold please stand up?" ______________

454. "I'll freeze, Bill!" ______________

455. "No, you can't choose the upper left square, the center square, or the lower left square. All those stars are dead." ______________

456. "It's a movie! One word! How many syllables?"
____

457. "It's not what you say that counts . . ." ______________
____

458. The quiz show created by Allan ("My Son, the Folksinger") Sherman and emceed by Gary Moore.________

459. The only quiz show that required a contestant to sign an affidavit.________

460. " 'Who' for $50, Art!"________

461. The quiz show that brought Dr. Joyce Brothers to fame.________

462. "75 . . . 125 . . . Devil!"________

463. "Gentlemen, which appliance best describes your wife during romance: a locked freezer, an uncontainable microwave, or a hot oven?"________

464. The quiz show that led Johnny Carson to *The Tonight Show*.________

465. No, this quiz show featuring Larry Hovis from *Hogan's Heroes* wasn't about the Nixon administration.________

Answers

446. *You Bet Your Life*
447. *The $25,000 Pyramid*
448. *What's My Line?*
449. *Password*
450. *The Dating Game*
451. *Jeopardy*
452. *Queen for a Day*
453. *To Tell the Truth*
454. *The* (original) *Price Is Right*
455. *Hollywood Squares*
456. *Stump the Stars*
457. *You Don't Say*
458. *I've Got a Secret*
459. *To Tell the Truth*
460. *The Who, What, and Where Game*
461. *The $64,000 Question*
462. *The Joker's Wild*
463. *The Newlywed Game*
464. *Who Do You Trust?*
465. *Liar's Club*

Take It for a Spin

Questions

Very often, a show is so successful or one of its characters so appealing that the network will spin off a brand new series. Match the spinoff to the show from which it was spun for 1 point each.

466. *Trapper John, M.D.*	*The Man from U.N.C.L.E.*
467. *Fish*	*Columbo*
468. *Pete and Gladys*	*Three's Company*
469. *Knots Landing*	*The Six Million Dollar Man*
470. *The Girl from U.N.C.L.E.*	*December Bride*
471. *Gomer Pyle, U.S.M.C.*	*Petticoat Junction*
472. *Benson*	*Diff'rent Strokes*
473. *Good Times*	*M*A*S*H*
474. *Richie Brockelman, Private Eye*	*Bewitched*
475. *The Facts of Life*	*Dallas*
476. *The Ropers*	*Alice*
477. *Green Acres*	*The Rockford Files*
478. *Flo*	*The Andy Griffith Show*
479. *Tabitha*	*Maude*
480. *The Bionic Woman*	*Soap*
481. *Kate Loves a Mystery*	*Barney Miller*

482. *For 3 Trivia Points* Name the three series spun out of *Happy Days*.

483. *For 3 Trivia Points* Name the three series spun out of *The Mary Tyler Moore Show*.

484. *For 3 Trivia Points* Name the three series spun out of *Sanford and Son*.

485. *For 4 Trivia Points* Name the four series spun directly out of *All in the Family*.

Answers

466. *M*A*S*H*
467. *Barney Miller*
468. *December Bride*
469. *Dallas*
470. *The Man from U. N. C. L. E.*
471. *The Andy Griffith Show*
472. *Soap*
473. *Maude*
474. *The Rockford Files*
475. *Diff'rent Strokes*
476. *Three's Company*
477. *Petticoat Junction*
478. *Alice*
479. *Bewitched*
480. *The Six Million Dollar Man*
481. *Columbo*
482. *Laverne and Shirley*, *Mork and Mindy*, and *Joanie Loves Chachi*
483. *Rhoda*, *Phyllis*, and *Lou Grant*
484. *The Sanford Arms*, *Grady*, and *Sanford*
485. *Maude*, *The Jeffersons*, *Archie Bunker's Place*, and *Gloria*

Munster Mish-Mash

Questions

The following is a list of cast members from The Munsters *and* The Addams Family. *Identify the show each actor or actress appeared in and the part he or she played. Each correctly filled-in blank is worth 1 trivia point.*

	SHOW	ROLE
486. Jackie Coogan	________	________
487. Lisa Loring	________	________
488. Pat Priest	________	________
489. Butch Patrick	________	________
490. John Astin	________	________
491. Fred Gwynne	________	________
492. Ted Cassidy	________	________
493. Al Lewis	________	________
494. Yvonne DeCarlo	________	________
495. Itself	________	________
496. Carolyn Jones	________	________
497. Ken Weatherwax	________	________
498. Blossom Rock	________	________
499. Felix Silla	________	________
500. Beverly Owen	________	________

486. *Addams Family* Uncle Fester
487. *Addams Family* Wednesday
488. *Munsters* Marilyn (second actress)
489. *Munsters* Eddie
490. *Addams Family* Gomez
491. *Munsters* Herman
492. *Addams Family* Lurch
493. *Munsters* Grandpa
494. *Munsters* Lily
495. *Addams Family* Thing
496. *Addams Family* Morticia
497. *Addams Family* Pugsley
498. *Addams Family* Grandma-ma
499. *Addams Family* Cousin Itt
500. *Munsters* Marilyn (original actress)

Answers

Gunsmoke

Questions

Each question about Marshal Dillon and his colleagues is worth 1 point.

Match the first name to the last name:

501. Matt	Adams
502. Kitty	Dillon
503. Chester	Haggen
504. Galen	Russell
505. Festus	Goode

506. In what city and state did *Gunsmoke* take place?

507. What was the name of Miss Kitty's saloon?

508. Burt Reynolds was a *Gunsmoke* co-star for years, playing the role of:
- a. Gunsmith Newly O'Brien
- b. Bartender Sam
- c. Drunkard Louis Pheeters
- d. Blacksmith Quint Asper
- e. Mortician Percy Crump

509. The actor who played Chester went on to star as:
- a. McCloud
- b. Kentucky Jones
- c. Grizzly Adams
- d. All of the above
- e. Both (a) and (b)

510. James Arness, the marshal in *Gunsmoke*, earlier portrayed a well-known monster in the movies. He was:

a. The Thing
b. The Blob
c. The Wolfman
d. Swamp Thing
e. The Creature from the Black Lagoon

Answers

501. Dillon
502. Russell
503. Goode
504. Adams
505. Haggen
506. Dodge City, Kansas
507. The Long Branch Saloon
508. (d) Blacksmith Quint Asper
509. (e) Both (a) and (b)—the actor was Dennis Weaver
510. (a) The Thing

A Sporting Proposition

Questions

Put some big points on the trivia scoreboard with correct answers about sports on TV. We'll give you 1 point for each correct response, but you'll have to supply your own Astroturf, Gatorade, and cheerleaders.

511. Before he teamed up with Joe Garagiola to do *NBC's Baseball Game of the Week*, Vin Scully was known as the voice of:

a. Firestone
b. Reason
c. Audrey Hepburn in *My Fair Lady*
d. The Yankees
e. The Dodgers

512. In 1984, ABC's team of announcers for *Monday Night Baseball* included a former manager, an underwear model, and a lawyer. Can you identify these three personalities?

513. One of the most memorable moments in sports happened at the 1980 winter Olympics when the U.S. hockey team beat the Russians. Who gained fame doing the play-by-play of that match?

514. Who was ABC's anchorman for the 1968, 1972, 1976, 1980 (winter), and 1984 Olympic games?

515. Which network televised the first Super Bowl in 1967?

516. What sport featured the San Francisco Bay Area Bombers, the New York Chiefs, and the Midwest Pioneers?

517. What football announcer won't fly on airplanes and bursts through the screen for Lite Beer from Miller?

518. One of the greatest blunders in televised sports occurred when NBC turned off the final two minutes of a thrilling seesaw battle between the New York Jets and the Oakland Raiders to show another program. What was it?

519. What show features "the thrill of victory, the agony of defeat?"

520. What cable network airs such sporting events as PKA full-contact karate, tractor pulls, and hydroplane racing to go along with games from the USFL, CFL, and NBA?

521. What sport was shown on prime-time network TV regularly from 1946 through 1964 and featured such announcers as Dennis James, Jack Drees, and Don Dunphy?

522. Who hosts *The Professional Bowlers Tour* on ABC?

523. Al McGuire and Billy Packer are color commentators for:

a. Championship wrestling
b. College football
c. College basketball
d. USFL football
e. NBA basketball

524. *TRIVIA UPDATE* From 1970 through 1984, eight men have regularly broadcast *Monday Night Football* for ABC. Name them for 1 point each.

525. What sport features announcers Vince McMahon and Gordon Solie and such managers as "Classy" Freddie Blassie, the Grand Wizard, and J. J. Dillion?

Answers

525. Wrestling

524. Howard Cosell, Dandy Don Meredith, and Frank Gifford are the perennials. Keith Jackson did the play-by-play in 1970. Alex Karras replaced Meredith from 1974 to 1976. In 1977 Don Meredith returned. Fran Tarkenton and O. J. Simpson have filled in occasionally since 1979. Fred "The Hammer" Williamson lasted only through the preseason in 1974.

523. (c) College basketball

522. Chris Schenkel

521. Boxing

520. ESPN

519. *ABC's Wide World of Sports*

518. A special of *Heidi*

517. Former coach and announcer *extraordinaire*, John Madden

516. The sport that dominated ABC's prime-time schedule in 1949 was roller derby.

515. Both CBS (with the rights to NFL games) and NBC (with AFL rights) televised that first Super Bowl.

514. Jim McKay

513. Al Michaels

512. Earl Weaver was the manager, Cy Young winner Jim Palmer the jockey shorts model, and Howard Cosell the lawyer.

511. (e) The Dodgers

Death and Taxis

Questions

One of the funniest situation comedies on the air during the late 1970s and early 1980s was Taxi. *You can hail* Taxi *by answering these questions for 1 point each and racking up a fare score.*

526. The name of the cab company on *Taxi* was:
- a. Fresh Air Cab Company
- b. Sunshine Cab Company
- c. Calloway Cab Company
- d. Income Taxis
- e. Yellow Cab Company

527. Latka Gravas, the foreign mechanic, got married to a woman named:
- a. Myasthenia
- b. Costa
- c. Cyndi
- d. Simca
- e. Nachas

528. One of the classic characters on *Taxi* was Reverend Jim, an ex-hippie whose brain had been fried in the 1960s. *FOR 2 TRIVIA POINTS* What was Jim's last name?

529. Who won an Emmy award for his portrayal of Reverend Jim?

530. What was the name of the bar where the cabbies hung out?

531. Louie DePalma, the dispatcher, was one of the nastiest and funniest characters ever to appear on TV. Name the diminutive actor who brought Louie to life.

532. Match the cabbies to their last names and other professions. You get 1 point for each correct match.

Elaine	a. Wheeler	i. Student
Bobby	b. Nardo	ii. Boxer
Tony	c. Burns	iii. Art gallery receptionist
John	d. Banta	iv. Actor

533. What was the first name of Louie's assistant dispatcher?

534. Louie had a kindhearted girlfriend, Zena, who was much too good for him. *FOR 2 TRIVIA POINTS* Who played Zena and on what show did the actress later land a regular role?

535. Alex Rieger was the center of sanity in the cab company. Alex's ex-wife was played by an actress who had earlier starred in her own series. Who was she?

a. Marilu Henner
b. Tammy Grimes
c. Linda Lavin
d. Louise Lasser
e. Mary Tyler Moore

Answers

526. (b) Sunshine Cab Company
527. (d) Simca
528. Ignatowski
529. Christopher Lloyd
530. Mario's
531. Danny DeVito
532. (b, iii) Elaine Nardo, art gallery receptionist, (a, iv) Bobby Wheeler, actor, (d, ii) Tony Banta, boxer, (c, i) John Burns, student
533. Jeff
534. Danny DeVito's wife, Rhea Perlman, was Zena before she became Carla, the waitress on *Cheers*.
535. (d) *Mary Hartman, Mary Hartman* star Louise Lasser

Name that Tune!

Questions

Answer these questions about hit songs from TV shows for 1 point each.

Match the hit theme to the show.

536. "Seattle"	*Dr. Kildare*
537. "Nadia's Theme"	*Dark Shadows*
538. "Making Our Dreams Come True"	*Angie*
539. "Believe It or Not"	*Here Come the Brides*
540. "Quentin's Theme"	*Have Gun, Will Travel*
541. "Keep Your Eye on the Sparrow"	*All in the Family*
542. "Different Worlds"	*Laverne and Shirley*
543. "Those Were the Days"	*Baretta*
544. "Three Stars Will Shine Tonight"	*The Greatest American Hero*
545. "Ballad of Paladin"	*The Young and the Restless*

546. Fess Parker sang "The Ballad of Davy Crockett" on *Disneyland* on December 15, 1954 and reached Number Five on the charts, but a longtime star of the soap opera *The Days of Our Lives* made it to Number One on the hit parade with his version of the song. Who is he?

547. Michael Parks had a hit in 1970 with "Long, Lonesome Highway." Name the TV series in which Parks starred and first sang that song.

548. Who had big hits with the themes to *The Rockford Files* and *Hill Street Blues*?

549. "Kookie, Kookie, Lend Me Your Comb" was a hit duet for stars from *77 Sunset Strip* and *Hawaiian Eye*. Who were they?

550. Surprisingly, at least four hit records came out of that all-American family sitcom *The Donna Reed Show*. Name the stars who sang these hits for 1 point each.

a. "My Dad"
b. "Johnny Angel"
c. "Good-by Cruel World"
d. "She Can't Find Her Keys"

551. *The Partridge Family* had its first Number One hit record in 1970. What was it?

552. Who had a hit in 1976 with the theme from *Happy Days*?

553. This song was on the charts longer than the show was on the air! Who had a Number Five hit in 1979 with the theme from *Makin' It*, a TV series inspired by *Saturday Night Fever*? (HINT: He was the star of the show.)

554. Who had hits with the themes to *S.W.A.T.* and *Baretta*?

555. The theme from *Mission: Impossible* was written and recorded by:

a. Henry Mancini
b. Nelson Riddle
c. Ricky Nelson
d. Lalo Schifrin
e. Earle Hagen

556. Who wrote the theme from *The Tonight Show*?

557. What was the theme song from *Make Room for Daddy*?

558. What is Bob Hope's theme song?

559. What was the theme song from *The Jack Benny Show*?

560. *Bosom Buddies'* theme song was once a hit record. Can you name it?

a. "A Day in the Life" by the Beatles
b. "That's Life" by Frank Sinatra
c. "My Life" by Billy Joel
d. "Where the Boys Are" by Connie Francis
e. "Standing on the Corner Watching All the Girls Go By" by the Four Lads

Answers

536. *Here Come the Brides*
537. *The Young and the Restless*
538. *Laverne and Shirley*
539. *The Greatest American Hero*
540. *Dark Shadows*
541. *Baretta*
542. *Angie*
543. *All in the Family*
544. *Dr. Kildare*
545. *Have Gun, Will Travel*
546. Bill Hayes
547. *Then Came Bronson*
548. Mike Post
549. Edd "Kookie" Byrnes of *77 Sunset Strip* and Connie Stevens of *Hawaiian Eye*
550. (a) Paul Petersen, (b) Shelley Fabares, (c) James Darren, (d) Paul Petersen
551. "I Think I Love You," which was also the Number Four record for the entire year!
552. Pratt and McClain
553. David Naughton, who was also the singing and dancing Pepper in all those Dr. Pepper commercials
554. Rhythm Heritage
555. (d) Lalo Schifrin
556. Paul Anka
557. "Danny Boy"
558. "Thanks for the Memories"
559. "Love in Bloom"
560. (c) "My Life" by Billy Joel

Animal House

Questions

Fill in the blank with the animal that completes the title of the TV series for 1 point each.

561. *The Iron* ________
562. ________ *Masterson*
563. *T.H.E.* ________
564. *B. J. and the* ________
565. *The* ________ *Factory*
566. *Air* ________
567. *The* ________ *Patrol*
568. *Leave It to* ________
569. *Me and the* ________
570. *Tales of the Gold* ________
571. ________ *Crest*
572. *The* ________ *Family*
573. *The* ________ (comedy about a rock group)
574. ________ *.45*
575. *The Life and Times of* ________ *Adams*
576. *The Chicago Teddy* ________
577. *The Black* ________ *Squadron*
578. ________ (starred Burt Reynolds)

579. __________ (starred Abe Vigoda)
580. __________ (starred Ty Hardin)
581. *The Amazing __________-Man*
582. *Top __________* (cartoon)
583. *__________man*
584. *The __________winkle Show*
585. *The __________ Club*
586. *Dan __________*
587. *Brave __________*
588. *The Bad News __________*
589. *__________boy in Africa*
590. *The Adventures of __________ Hood*

Answers

561. Horse
562. Bat
563. Cat
564. Bear
565. Duck
566. Wolf
567. Rat
568. Beaver
569. Chimp
570. Monkey
571. Falcon
572. Partridge
573. Monkees
574. Colt
575. Grizzly
576. Bears
577. Sheep
578. Hawk
579. Fish
580. Bronco
581. Spider
582. Cat
583. Bat
584. Bull
585. Stork
586. Raven
587. Eagle
588. Bears
589. Cow
590. Robin

Who Am I?

Questions

Answer these IDs correctly after Clue A for 5 points, after Clue B for 3 points, or after Clue C for 1 point.

591. A. I was *The Range Rider.*
B. I was also *Yancy Derringer.*
C. People still remember me best as one of moviedom's Tarzans.
My name is ______________________.

592. A. I was Ben Richards, *The Immortal.*
B. I was better known as Sergeant Sam Troy on *The Rat Patrol.*
C. I was best known as the husband of Linda Day.
My name was ______________________.

593. A. I was Heather Finch, an exchange student from England, on *Fair Exchange.*
B. I was Julie Willis, a young married artist, on *Love on a Rooftop.*
C. I was *Laugh-In*'s Sock-It-to-Me Girl.
My name is ______________________.

594. A. I was Seaman Happy Haines on *McHale's Navy.*
B. I was Murray Slaughter on *The Mary Tyler Moore Show.*
C. I'm Captain Merrill Steubing on *The Love Boat.*
My name is ________________________.

595. A. I was Alf Monroe, a carpenter who teamed up with his sister Ralph. We were called the Monroe Brothers on *Green Acres.*
B. I was sidekick Ikky Mudd on *Captain Midnight.*
C. I was Charley Halper on *The Danny Thomas Show.*
My name is ________________________.

Answers

591. Jock Mahoney
592. Christopher George
593. Judy Carne
594. Gavin MacLeod
595. Sid Melton

Dual Identity

Questions

Identify the following TV performers from these appellations for 2 trivia points each.

596. The TW3 Girl
597. The Sock-It-to-Me Girl
598. Mr. Television
599. The Great Stoneface
600. The Continental
601. Ukulele Ike
602. Her Nibs
603. The Champagne Lady
604. The Hullabaloo Girl (or The Girl in the Cage)
605. The Ghostess with the Mostest
606. That Most Sporting Spirit
607. The Surly Surgeon
608. Kookie
609. The Old Ranger
610. Captain Kangaroo

Answers

596. Nancy Ames
597. Judy Carne
598. Milton Berle
599. Ed Sullivan
600. Renzo Cesana
601. Cliff Edwards
602. Georgia Gibbs
603. Alice Lon
604. Lada Edmund Jr.
605. Anne Jeffreys (as Marion Kirby)
606. Robert Sterling (as George Kirby)
607. Vince Edwards (as Ben Casey)
608. Edd Byrnes
609. Stanley Andrews
610. Bob Keeshan

Potpourri Quiz

Questions

Answer these toughies for 2 trivia points each.

611. Who was Abbott and Costello's landlord?

612. True or False. Martin Milner and Kent McCord were the stars of *Route 66*.

613. What was the name of Johnny Quest's dog?

a. Race
b. Hadji
c. Bandit
d. Rex
e. Buttons

614. Whose address was 822 Sycamore Road, Hillsdale?

615. Which cavalry adopted Rusty and his dog Rin Tin Tin?

a. 101st
b. 7th
c. 4,077th
d. 3rd
e. 54th

616. Leonardo was the whispering, scientific sidekick to whom?

617. *The Americans* was a 1961 show about two brothers fighting on different sides during the Civil War. Darryl Hickman played the Union soldier named ________ and Dick Davidson played his Confederate brother, ________.

618. In what state would you find the town of Mayberry?

619. Who were the two stars of *Anna and the King*?

620. On what TV show did Don Porter play Mr. Devery, the manager of the Bartley House Hotel?

621. Which city was *The Asphalt Jungle*?

622. Who lived at Number Three, Stable Mews, London?

623. Whose boyfriend was Howard Meechim?

624. Between *Star Trek* and *T. J. Hooker*, William Shatner starred in another TV series. What was it?

625. Who ran the 12th Precinct in New York?

626. Who provided the voices of the Beatles on *The Beatles* cartoon show?

627. Who was Daisy Moses of 518 Crestview Drive, Beverly Hills, California?

628. Who was the top exec with McMann and Tate?

629. How many "Bicentennial Minutes" were there?

Match the first and last names of these characters from The Bob Newhart Show.

630. Bob	Borden
631. Howard	Hartley
632. Jerry	Kester
633. Carol	Carlin
634. Elliott	Robinson

635. What was the meaning of the title of the TV show *Broken Arrow*?

636. What was Billy Bang Bang's brother's name?

637. The creators of *Amos 'n' Andy* later had a cartoon show directly inspired by their famous characters. Name the show.

638. On what show would you expect to find Dancing Bear, Bunny Rabbit, and Grandfather Clock?

639. Who were Gunther and Francis?

640. Who were Mr. Rodriguez and Mr. Brown?

Answers

611. Sidney Fields
612. False. They were the stars of *Adam-12*.
613. (c) Bandit
614. Ozzie and Harriet Nelson
615. (a) 101st
616. Clyde Crashcup
617. Ben Canfield; Jeff Canfield
618. North Carolina
619. Yul Brynner and Samantha Eggar
620. *The Ann Sothern Show*
621. New York City
622. John Steed on *The Avengers*
623. Kelly Gregg on *Bachelor Father*
624. *The Barbary Coast*
625. *Barney Miller*
626. Paul Frees was the voice of both John and George; Lance Percival put words in Paul's and Ringo's mouths.
627. Granny on *The Beverly Hillbillies*
628. Darrin Stevens on *Bewitched*
629. 732
630. Hartley
631. Borden
632. Robinson
633. Kester
634. Carlin
635. It was the Indian peace symbol.
636. Butch Bang Bang
637. *Calvin and the Colonel*
638. *Captain Kangaroo*
639. Gunther Toody and Francis Muldoon on *Car 54, Where Are You?*
640. *Chico and the Man*

That's Unanswerable!

Questions

If real men don't eat quiche, what don't Real People do? They don't shout "That's Incredible!" when we ask them to identify the hosts of TV's various "reality" programs. Be careful not to make any bloopers, foul-ups, or bleeps when you tell us, for 1 point apiece, on which of the following TV shows each TV personality was a regular:

Real People; *TV's Bloopers and Practical Jokes*; *That's Incredible!*; *Foul-Ups, Bleeps, and Blunders*; *Speak Up, America!*; *People*; and *Those Amazing Animals*.

641. Dick Clark
642. Phyllis George
643. Jayne Kennedy
644. Fran Tarkenton
645. Skip Stephenson
646. Fred Willard
647. Don Rickles
648. Ed McMahon
649. Priscilla Presley
650. John Davidson
651. Mark Russell
652. Marjoe Gortner
653. Sarah Purcell
654. Cathy Lee Crosby
655. Rhonda Bates
656. Byron Allen
657. Burgess Meredith
658. Bill Rafferty
659. Jim Stafford
660. John Barbour

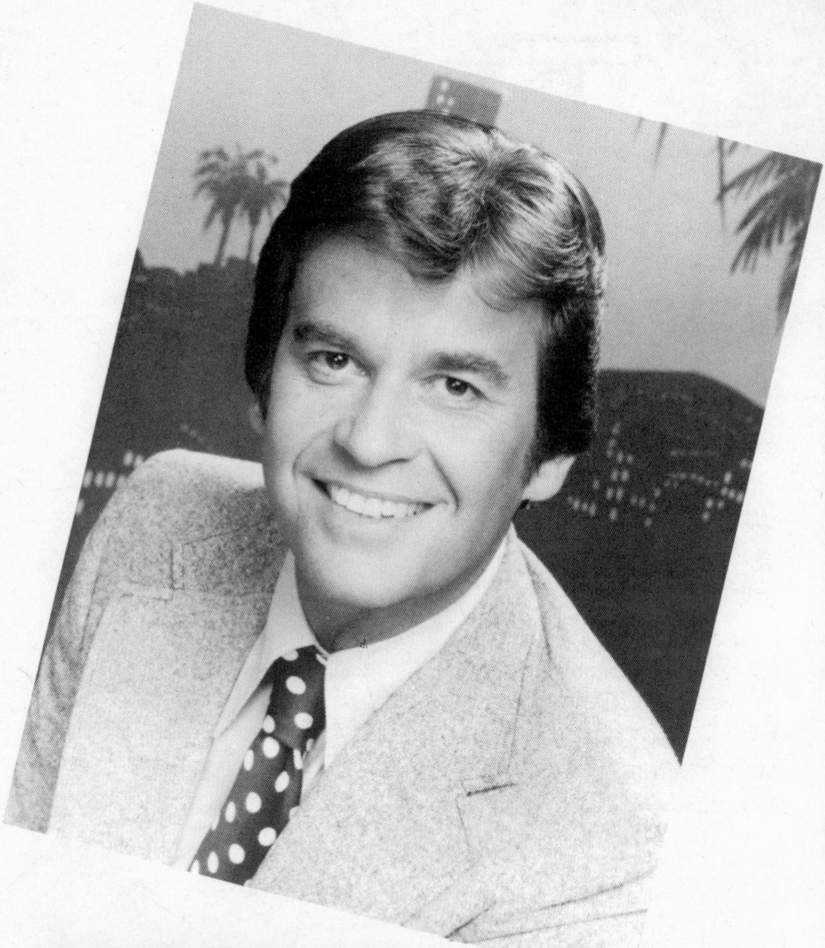

Answers

641. TV's Bloopers and Practical Jokes
642. People
643. Speak Up, America!
644. That's Incredible!
645. Real People
646. Real People
647. Foul-Ups, Bleeps, and Blunders
648. TV's Bloopers and Practical Jokes
649. Those Amazing Animals
650. That's Incredible!
651. Real People
652. Speak Up, America!
653. Real People
654. That's Incredible!
655. Speak Up, America!
656. Real People
657. Those Amazing Animals
658. Real People
659. Those Amazing Animals
660. Real People

Disney Stuff

Questions

Each Disney question from the wonderful world of trivia is worth 1 point.

661. Disney became "synful" in 1958 with the adventures of a colonial hero named Dr. Syn. The good doctor was better known as:

a. The Swamp Fox
b. Zorro
c. The Scarecrow
d. The Love Bug
e. The Son of Liberty

662. Dr. Syn was played by:

a. Patrick MacNee
b. Patrick McGoohan
c. Patrick O'Neal
d. Patrick O'Brien
e. Patrick Brady

663. "Swamp Fox, Swamp Fox, tail on his hat . . ." What is the next line of this theme song?

664. "The Swamp Fox" was the nickname of a colonial colonel named:

a. Leslie Nielsen
b. Francis Marion
c. Francis Farmer
d. Francis Coppola
e. Harlan Sanders

665. What does "El Zorro" mean?

666. Zorro operated out of two California cities. In one he rode a black horse named Tornado and in the other he rode a white steed named Phantom. What were the two cities?

667. John Slaughter had a nickname too. It was:

a. New Jersey John Slaughter
b. Tombstone John Slaughter
c. Gentleman John Slaughter
d. Tennessee John Slaughter
e. Texas John Slaughter

668. John Slaughter attracted a lot of attention because he always wore two items *backwards*. What were they?

669. How many lives did Elfego Baca have?

670. Robert Loggia, who played Elfego Baca, returned to weekly TV years later as the star of a TV series. What was it?

671. In what direction did Andy Burnett always travel?

672. Who was Davy Crockett's companion and who played him?

673. What did TV frontiersmen Davy Crockett and Daniel Boone have in common?

674. When did Davy Crockett kill him a b'ar?

675. After Old Yeller saved everyone in the family time and again, what did his grateful owners do in return?

676. Which cartoon character opened the Disney show each week?

677. Which cartoon character always presented musical lessons on safety, science, and letting your conscience be your guide?

678. What was the name of the kid who had adventures in Pop Warner Football and Little League Baseball?

679. Disney climaxed his TV tour of Disneyland by putting a camera on the park's roller coaster so that viewers felt they were experiencing the ride. Name that roller coaster.

680. Which Mouseketeer apparently wore a bra, dragging a generation of kids into puberty as they watched their TV sets in awe?

Answers

661. (c) The Scarecrow
662. (b) Patrick McGoohan
663. "Nobody knows where the Swamp Fox's at."
664. (b) Francis Marion
665. The Fox
666. Los Angeles and Monterey
667. (e) Texas John Slaughter
668. His cowboy hat and his guns
669. Nine
670. *T.H.E. Cat*
671. West
672. George Russel, played by Buddy Ebsen
673. Both were portrayed by Fess Parker
674. When he was only three
675. Shot him smack between the eyes
676. Tinkerbelle
677. Jiminy Cricket
678. Moochie
679. The Matterhorn
680. Annette (Funicello)

Baby Boomers

Questions

Here are stars and characters from famous TV kid shows. Name the program each appeared on for 1 trivia point apiece.

681. Don Herbert and a child assistant
682. Mr. Greenjeans and Grandfather Clock
683. Beulah Witch and Madame Ooglepuss
684. Karen and Cubby
685. Inspector Henderson and Miss Baccarat
686. Froggy the Gremlin and Gunga Ram
687. Chief Thunderthud and Mr. Bluster
688. Lamb Chop and Hush Puppy
689. Pinhead and Foodini
690. Gala Poochie and Polka Dottie
691. Joey and Pete
692. Sonny Fox
693. Jack Barry
694. Miss Francis
695. Al and Wanda Lewis
696. Mary Hartline and Claude Kirchner

697. Big Tim Champion and Corky
698. White Fang and Black Tooth
699. Pookie and Peaches
700. Hobart and Reba

Answers

681. *Mr. Wizard*
682. *Captain Kangaroo*
683. *Kukla, Fran, and Ollie*
684. *The Mickey Mouse Club*
685. *Superman*
686. *Andy's Gang*
687. *Howdy Doody*
688. *The Shari Lewis Show*
689. *Lucky Pup*
690. *Rootie Kazootie*
691. *Fury*
692. *Wonderama* (or *Let's Take a Trip* or *On Your Mark*)
693. *Winky Dink*
694. *Ding Dong School*
695. *Uncle Al*
696. *Super Circus*
697. *Circus Boy*
698. *Soupy Sales*
699. *Soupy Sales*
700. *Soupy Sales*

I Ain't Afraid of No Hosts!

Questions

Identify the emcee of the following quiz shows for 1 trivia point each.

701. *Balance Your Budget*; *Double or Nothing*; *Break the Bank*; *Stop the Music*; *Bid 'n' Buy*; *Masquerade Party*

____

702. *PDQ*; *Haggis Baggis*; *High Finance*; *People Will Talk*; *Cash and Carry*; *On Your Account*

____

703. *Dollar a Second*; *Treasure Hunt*; *Songs for Sale*

____

704. *Dotto*; *Seven Keys*; *Video Village*

____

705. *Say When*; *Who, What, and Where Game*; *It's Academic*

____

Answers

701. Bert Parks
702. Dennis James
703. Jan Murray
704. Jack Narz
705. Art James

The Dallas Dynasty

Questions

Prime-time soaps such as Dallas, Dynasty, *and* Falcon Crest *are sudsing all over the airwaves. You can really clean up if you answer each question correctly for 1 point apiece.*

706. What do J. R. Ewing's initials stand for?

707. Name the two actresses who have played Miss Ellie.

708. Which of these Ewing women did not marry into the family?

a. Sue Ellen
b. Ellie
c. Lucy
d. Pam
e. All of the above

709. What was the name of the Ewing ranch?

710. Cliff Barnes's sister is played by:
a. Audrey Landers
b. Susan Howard
c. Victoria Principal
d. Victoria Wisdom
e. Susan Sullivan

711. Who shot J. R.?

712. Sue Ellen had a sister who had an affair with J. R. She was portrayed by:
a. Mary Crosby
b. Morgan Brittany
c. Morgan Fairchild
d. Priscilla Presley
e. Melinda Mays

713. Bobby Ewing had a half-brother named:
a. J. R.
b. Ray
c. Cliff
d. Jock
e. Itch

714. The star of *Falcon Crest* was married to:
a. A president of the United States
b. A grade B actor
c. The host of *Death Valley Days*
d. A governor of California
e. All of the above

715. What does Blake Carrington's wife have in common with Victoria Barkley's daughter Audra?

716. Name the actor who originated the role of Stephen Carrington on *Dynasty*.

717. Blake's majordomo was named:
a. John
b. George
c. Paul
d. Ringo
e. Joseph

718. Which of the following had a fatal heart attack during sex with Alexis Carrington?
a. Cecil
b. Jeff
c. Mark
d. Adam
e. The Green Bay Packers

719. Adam and Alexis drove Jeff crazy by spiking:
a. His drink
b. His volleyball
c. His wife
d. His underwear
e. The paint on his walls

720. In what city is Carrington Oil based?

721. What did Fallon and Kirby have in common?

722. Who was the first black actress to be a regular on *Dynasty*?

723. Mark, the tennis pro, was romantically involved with:

a. Crystal
b. Fallon
c. Alexis
d. Crystal, Fallon, and Alexis
e. Stephen

724. Heather Locklear played Stephen's vile wife. Her name was:

a. Sammy Spear
b. Bobby Jo
c. Joe Ed
d. Sarah Rose
e. Sammy Jo

725. Kirby's real father was:

a. Blake
b. Joseph
c. J. R. Ewing
d. Durwood
e. Grant

Answers

706. John Ross
707. Barbara Bel Geddes and Donna Reed
708. (c) Lucy
709. Southfork
710. (c) Victoria Principal
711. Kristen, Sue Ellen's sister
712. (a) Mary Crosby
713. (b) Ray
714. (e) All of the above
715. Both were portrayed by Linda Evans
716. Al Corley
717. (e) Joseph
718. (a) Cecil
719. (e) The paint on his walls
720. Denver
721. Both were married to Jeff.
722. Diahann Carroll
723. (d) Crystal, Fallon, and Alexis
724. (e) Sammy Jo
725. (b) Joseph

Yours, Mine, and Ours

Questions

Each of the following titles begins with the word Your, My, *or* Our. *Win 1 trivia point for each correctly filled-in blank.*

726. __________ *All-American College Show*
727. __________ *World and Welcome to It*
728. __________ *First Impression*
729. __________ *Living Doll*
730. __________ *Hit Parade*
731. __________ *Favorite Husband*
732. __________ *Show of Shows*
733. __________ *Man Higgins*
734. __________ *Three Sons*
735. __________ *Mother, the Car*
736. __________ *Favorite Martian*
737. __________ *Miss Brooks*
738. __________ *Partner the Ghost*
739. __________ *Son Jeep*
740. __________ *Private World*
741. __________ *Friend Flicka*

742. ________ *Friend Irma*
743. ________ *Friend Tony*
744. ________ *Surprise Package*
745. ________ *Little Margie*

Answers

726. Your
727. My
728. Your
729. My
730. Your
731. My
732. Your
733. Our
734. My
735. My
736. My
737. Our
738. My
739. My
740. Our
741. My
742. My
743. My
744. Your
745. My

Line-Ups

Questions

We'll give you a network's prime-time lineup of shows and you name the night of the week they were on for 1 point each.

746. *Happy Days*; *Laverne and Shirley*; *Three's Company*; *Soap*; *Family*

---

747. *Rhoda*; *Phyllis*; *All in the Family*; *Maude*; *Medical Center*

---

748. *Sanford and Son*; *Chico and the Man*; *The Rockford Files*; *Police Woman*

---

749. *All in the Family*; *M*A*S*H*; *The Mary Tyler Moore Show*; *The Bob Newhart Show*; *The Carol Burnett Show*

---

750. *The Monkees*; *The Man From U.N.C.L.E.*; *The Danny Thomas Show*; *I Spy*

---

751. *Shindig*; *The King Family Show*; *The Lawrence Welk Show*; *The Hollywood Palace*

---

752. *Mr. Ed*; *Lassie*; *My Favorite Martian*; *The Ed Sullivan Show*; *The Judy Garland Show*; *Candid Camera*; *What's My Line?*

---

753. *The Bell Telephone Hour*; *Walt Disney*; *Branded*; *Bonanza*; *The Wackiest Ship in the Army*

---

754. *To Tell the Truth*; *I've Got a Secret*; *The Lucy Show*; *The Danny Thomas Show*; *The Andy Griffith Show*; *East Side, West Side*

---

755. *Perry Mason*; *The Defenders*; *Have Gun, Will Travel*; *Gunsmoke*

---

756. *Leave It to Beaver*; *Zorro*; *The Real McCoys*; *The Pat Boone Show*; *Rough Riders*; *Traffic Court*

---

757. *Robin Hood*; *The Burns and Allen Show*; *Arthur Godfrey's Talent Scouts*; *I Love Lucy*; *December Bride*; *Studio One*

---

758. *The Waltons*; *Hawaii Five-O*; *Barnaby Jones*

---

759. *The Flintstones*; *The Donna Reed Show*; *My Three Sons*; *Bewitched*; *Peyton Place*; *The Jimmy Dean Show*

---

760. *The Wild Wild West*; *Hogan's Heroes*; *Gomer Pyle U.S.M.C.*; *The Smothers Brothers Show*; *Slattery's People*

---

761. *Batman*; *The Flying Nun*; *Bewitched*; *That Girl*; *Peyton Place*; *Good Company*

---

762. *The Brady Bunch*; *The Partridge Family*; *Room 222*; *The Odd Couple*; *Love American Style*

---

763. *Name That Tune*; *You'll Never Get Rich*; *Navy Log*; *Meet Millie*; *The Red Skelton Show*; *The $64,000 Question*; *My Favorite Husband*

---

764. *The Dinah Shore Show*; *The John Cameron Swayze News*; *The Milton Berle Show*; *Fireside Theater*; *Armstrong Circle Theater*; *Judge for Yourself*; *Bob Considine*; *It Happened in Sports*

---

765. *Welcome Back, Kotter*; *Barney Miller*; *The Tony Randall Show*; *The Nancy Walker Show*; *The Streets of San Francisco*

Answers

746. Tuesday
747. Monday
748. Friday
749. Saturday
750. Monday
751. Saturday
752. Sunday
753. Sunday
754. Monday
755. Saturday
756. Thursday
757. Monday
758. Thursday
759. Thursday
760. Friday
761. Thursday
762. Friday
763. Tuesday
764. Tuesday
765. Thursday

Go West, Young Man

Questions

Out of the blue of the Western sky comes our quiz about one of TV's most popular genres, the Western. Saddle your ponies, here we go for 1 point per correct answer. And smile when you say that, pardner!

766. A classic TV Western was *Maverick*. Who played Bret Maverick; his brother, Bart; and their cousin, Beau?

767. *Wanted: Dead or Alive* was the story of bounty hunter Josh Randall. What famous actor played Josh Randall?

768. Josh Randall carried a special gun, a sawed-off .30-40 carbine. What did he call his gun?

769. On *The Life and Legend of Wyatt Earp*, Marshal Earp also used a unique kind of gun that became his trademark. What was it?

770. Lucas McCain carried a special gun too—a modified Winchester with a large ring that let him fire as quickly as he drew. What title did this earn Lucas?

771. Match the actor to his role.

a.	Clint Walker	Bronco
b.	Ty Hardin	Cheyenne
c.	Will Hutchins	Sugarfoot

772. What was the name of the rotund soldier who was always bedeviled by the fox so cunning and free in *Zorro*?

773. What was Zorro's other identity?

774. The three sons on *Bonanza* were Adam, Hoss, and Little Joe. What was Hoss's real first name?

775. What did Hop Sing, Wishbone, and Charley Wooster have in common?

776. Who were the blood brothers on *Broken Arrow*?

777. What was the name of the newspaper edited by Harris Claibourne on *Tombstone Territory*?

778. Who came to fame wearing a coonskin cap?

a. Texas John Slaughter
b. The Swamp Fox
c. Andy Burnett
d. Davy Crockett
e. Elfego Baca

779. Who claimed he cut his teeth on a branding iron?

780. Who were adopted by Lieutenant Rip Masters, Sergeant Biff O'Hara, and the other soldiers of Fort Apache?

781. Who was called "the bravest, strongest, fightingest U.S. marshal in the whole West" by his sidekick, Jingles?

782. Marked with a white chess knight, what did Paladin's business card read?

783. Who were Barbara Stanwyck's four children on *The Big Valley* and who played them?

784. Before he took up broiling hamburgers, Roy Rogers was known as "The King of the Cowboys." Rogers rode Trigger. What did his sidekick, Patrick Aloysius Brady, ride?

785. "Hey Cisco!" "Hey Pancho!" In *The Cisco Kid*, who played "The Robin Hood of the Old West" and who was his sidekick, Pancho?

786. *Gunsmoke* ran for 20 years in prime time on CBS. During all that time, Marshal Matt Dillon had only two deputies. Can you name them?

787. True or False. William Conrad, who played the overweight detective Frank Cannon, was the original Marshal Matt Dillon when *Gunsmoke* started out on radio.

788. On *The Adventures of Kit Carson*, the frontier scout had a Mexican sidekick called:

a. Pancho
b. Bernardo
c. El Taco
d. El Toro
e. El Emenopee

789. True or False. Gabby Hayes starred in the hit Western *Frontier Rabbi*.

790. What TV Western has had two fast-food restaurant chains named after it?

Answers

766. Bret was played by James Garner, Bart by Jack Kelly, and Beau by Roger Moore.
767. Steve McQueen
768. Mare's Leg
769. His "Buntline Specials"—a pair of .45 pistols with extra-long barrels
770. *The Rifleman*
771. (a) Clint Walker—Cheyenne Bodie, (b) Ty Hardin—Bronco Layne, (c) Will Hutchins—Tom "Sugarfoot" Brewster
772. Sergeant Garcia
773. Don Diego de la Vega
774. Eric
775. They were all cooks—on *Bonanza, Rawhide*, and *Wagon Train* respectively.
776. Indian agent Tom Jeffords and Apache Chief Cochise
777. *The Tombstone Epitaph*
778. (d) Davy Crockett
779. Pete, the ranch hand, on *Fury*
780. Rusty and his dog Rin Tin Tin
781. Wild Bill Hickock
782. "Have Gun, Will Travel . . . Wire Paladin, San Francisco."
783. Richard Long was Jarrod Barkley; Peter Breck was Nick; Lee Majors was the illegitimate son, Heath; and Linda Evans was Audra.
784. Nelliebelle—a jeep
785. Duncan Renaldo was Cisco and Leo Carrillo was Pancho.
786. Chester Goode, played by Dennis Weaver, was Mister Dillon's limping sidekick from 1955 through 1964. Ken Curtis, as Festus Haggen, covered Dillon's rear from 1964 until 1975.
787. True. The thought of Conrad in chaps, leaping onto a horse, was so frightening that James Arness was given the role on TV.
788. (d) El Toro
789. False
790. No, it isn't *Rawhide*. *Bonanza* inspired both the Bonanza Steak House and the Ponderosa Steak House chains.

. . . and Jerry Mathers as the Beaver

Questions

These tough Leave It to Beaver *questions are worth 2 trivia points each.*

791. What was the Cleavers' address?

792. What was Ward's occupation?

793. What does *Leave It to Beaver* have in common with *Star Trek*?

794. Violet Rutherford, Lumpy's little sister, was played by an actress whose sister was playing Linda on *Make Room for Daddy* during the same period. Name both actresses.

795. Which of Beaver's friends had the last name Whitney?

a. Larry
b. Whitey
c. Gilbert
d. Benjie
e. Zeke

796. Name Beaver's female teacher.

797. Who was the old fire chief who always had advice for the Beaver?

798. Who was the girl universally despised by Beaver and his friends?

799. Who was Wally's girlfriend?

800. Fred Rutherford from *Leave It to Beaver* and Mel Cooley from *The Dick Van Dyke Show* were both portrayed by:

a. Richard Deacon
b. Morey Amsterdam
c. Carl Reiner
d. Frank Bank
e. Ken Osmond

Answers

791. 211 Pine Street, Mayfield
792. Accountant
793. Majel Barrett, who played Mrs. Rutherford on *Leave It to Beaver*, also played Nurse Chappell on *Star Trek*.
794. Veronica and Angela Cartwright
795. (b) Whitey
796. Miss Landers
797. Gus
798. Judy Hessler
799. Julie Foster
800. (a) Richard Deacon

From TV Screen to Silver Screen

Questions

Some of Hollywood's most famous actors and actresses started out in TV series before finding fame and fortune in the movies. For 1 point each, match the actor to the TV series associated with his or her early career.

801.	Debra Winger	*Gidget*
802.	Warren Beatty	*Johnny Staccato*
803.	Raquel Welch	*Peyton Place*
804.	John Travolta	*The Pride of the Family*
805.	Jamie Lee Curtis	*Saturday Night Live*
806.	Jack Lemmon	*Klondike*
807.	Goldie Hawn	*The Green Hornet*
808.	John Cassavetes	*The Texas Wheelers*
809.	Gena Rowlands	*Welcome Back, Kotter*
810.	Mark Hamill	*That Wonderful Guy*
811.	Natalie Wood	*Wonder Woman*
812.	James Coburn	*Stoney Burke*
813.	Jodie Foster	*Rowan and Martin's Laugh-In*
814.	Jeff Goldblum	*The Second Hundred Years*
815.	Sally Field	*Tenspeed and Brown Shoe*
816.	Bruce Lee	*Dobie Gillis*
817.	Karen Black	*Operation Petticoat*
818.	Bruce Dern	*Paper Moon*
819.	Mia Farrow	*87th Precinct*
820.	Eddie Murphy	*The Hollywood Palace*

Answers

801. *Wonder Woman*
802. *Dobie Gillis*
803. *The Hollywood Palace*
804. *Welcome Back, Kotter*
805. *Operation Petticoat*
806. *That Wonderful Guy*
807. *Rowan and Martin's Laugh-In*
808. *Johnny Staccato*
809. *87th Precinct*
810. *The Texas Wheelers*
811. *The Pride of the Family*
812. *Klondike*
813. *Paper Moon*
814. *Tenspeed and Brown Shoe*
815. *Gidget*
816. *The Green Hornet*
817. *The Second Hundred Years*
818. *Stoney Burke*
819. *Peyton Place*
820. *Saturday Night Live*

The Fumblers

Questions

Name the actors who starred as these comical, clumsy, fumbling characters for 2 trivia points each.

821. Rango______________________________
822. Captain Nice__________________________
823. Mr. Terrific__________________________
824. Maxwell Smart________________________
825. Captain Parmenter_____________________
826. Ensign Parker________________________
827. Dagwood Bumstead_____________________
828. Chester Riley_________________________
829. Gilligan_____________________________
830. Sugarfoot____________________________

Answers

821. Tim Conway
822. William Daniels
823. Stephen Strimpell
824. Don Adams
825. Ken Berry
826. Tim Conway
827. Arthur Lake or Will Hutchins
828. William Bendix or Jackie Gleason
829. Bob Denver
830. Will Hutchins

M.D. TV

Questions

The following is a list of 25 TV shows about doctors and nurses. From this list, for 1 point apiece, select the one that corresponds most closely to the TV Guide*-type descriptions below.*

Ben Casey
Dr. Kildare
The Nurses
Doctor in the House
Temperature's Rising
The Interns
Doctor's Hospital
Quincy, M.E.
*M*A*S*H*
The Doctors (The Bold Ones)
Nurse
Marcus Welby, M.D.
St. Elsewhere
Emergency!
Medical Story
General Hospital
Doc Corkle
Lifeline
Medic
The Eleventh Hour
Daktari
Medical Center
Doc Elliot
Doc
Having Babies

831. Mama Walton turns in her children for a nurse's license and goes to work in a big city hospital. ________

832. The medical profession's answer to *Hill Street Blues*. ________

833. Now that the Cleaver family has moved out, Consuelo puts up a sign with the names of Dr. Steve Kiley and her boss. ________

834. The camera follows real-life doctors through one medical crisis after another.____________________

835. County General is abuzz with reports that both Dr. Zorba and his favorite resident were seen smiling.

____

836. Julie Farr, M.D., uses Federal Express to ensure the overnight delivery of a baby who absolutely, positively has to be there the next day. ____________________

837. Dr. Marsh Tracy reprimands a patient who has the manners of a baboon and, in fact, is one.________

838. Dr. Joe Bogart cares for his disadvantaged patients out of love for them and his profession instead of love for the dollar.________

839. Medical hi-jinx abound with Cleavon Little from *Blazing Saddles*, later joined by Paul Lynde from *The Hollywood Squares*.________

840. David Hartman as Dr. Paul Hunter loses so many patients that E. G. Marshall, as his boss Dr. Ben Craig, tells him he'll have to host a new show called *Good Mourning, America*.________

841. Much to the distress of Dr. Paul Lochner, Dr. Joe Gannon again becomes personally involved in the lives of his patients.________

842. Have Scalpel, Will Travel. Wire Dr. Konrad Styner, Los Angeles.________

843. The misadventures of Dr. Pierce and Dr. MacIntyre continue.________

844. The paramedics of Squad 51 rush from here to there (as usual).________

845. Psychiatrist Dr. Theodore Bassett, played by Wendell Corey, takes us on another mental case.________

846. The adventures of two doctors—Jim, and his adviser, Leonard Gillespie.________

847. Presenting the world's only doctor who seemingly has no first name.________

848. A big city doctor takes his practice to the backwoods of Colorado.________

849. England's racy comedy about zany med students in London.________

850. Luke and Laura continue to draw attention away from the medical stories in this daytime soap.________

851. When Mike Farrell (B. J. of *M**A**S**H*) was younger, he played intern Dr. Sam Marsh and had to report to Broderick Crawford as Dr. Peter Goldstone instead of to Harry Morgan as Colonel Sherman Potter.

____

852. At New York's Alden General Hospital, head nurse Liz Thorpe (Shirl Conway) chews out nurse Gail Lucas (Zina Bethune).________

853. Before joining *The A-Team*, George Peppard joined Lowell Memorial Hospital as Dr. Jake Goodwin.________

____

854. The medical profession's answer to such anthology-style series as *Police Story*. ________

855. America braces itself for a biting comedy about a dentist, starring Eddie Mayehoff.________

Answers

831. *Nurse*
832. *St. Elsewhere*
833. *Marcus Welby, M.D.*
834. *Lifeline*
835. *Ben Casey*
836. *Having Babies*
837. *Daktari*
838. *Doc*
839. *Temperature's Rising*
840. *The Doctors (The Bold Ones)*
841. *Medical Center*
842. *Medic*
843. *M**A**S**H*
844. *Emergency!*
845. *The Eleventh Hour*
846. *Dr. Kildare*
847. *Quincy, M.E.*
848. *Doc Elliot*
849. *Doctor in the House*
850. *General Hospital*
851. *The Interns*
852. *The Nurses*
853. *Doctor's Hospital*
854. *Medical Story*
855. *Doc Corkle*

Char-Actresses

Questions

Now it's time for the ladies. We'll give you the names of three characters and you tell us which actress played all three for 1 point each.

856. ____________________ Lucy Carter, Lucy Carmichael, Lucy Ricardo

857. ____________________ Jill Danko, Sabrina Duncan, Amanda King

858. ____________________ Marty Shaw, Audra Barkley, Krystle Jennings Carrington

859. ____________________ Peggy Maxwell, Sally McMillan, Kate McArdle

860. ____________________ Myrna Turner, Janice Dreyfuss, Laverne DeFazio

861. ____________________ Bridget Fitzgerald Steinberg, Nancy Lawrence Maitland, Elyse Keaton

862. ____________________ Liza Hammond, Eve Hubbard, Connie Brooks

863. ____________________ Mildred the Maid, Nancy Blansky, Ida Morgenstern

864. ____________________ Jenny Bedford, Dr. Anne Jamison, Mary Stone

865. ________________ Miriam Welby, Ellie Walker, Betty Anderson

866. ________________ Lisa Benton, Pam Davidson, Christine Francis

867. ________________ Penny Alston, Nurse Kathleen Faverty, Christine Cagney

868. ________________ Toni "Feather" Danton, April Dancer, Jennifer Hart

869. ________________ Katy O'Connor, Susie McNamera, Gladys Crabtree (a 1928 Porter)

870. ________________ Loco Jones, Stella Johnson, Jeannie

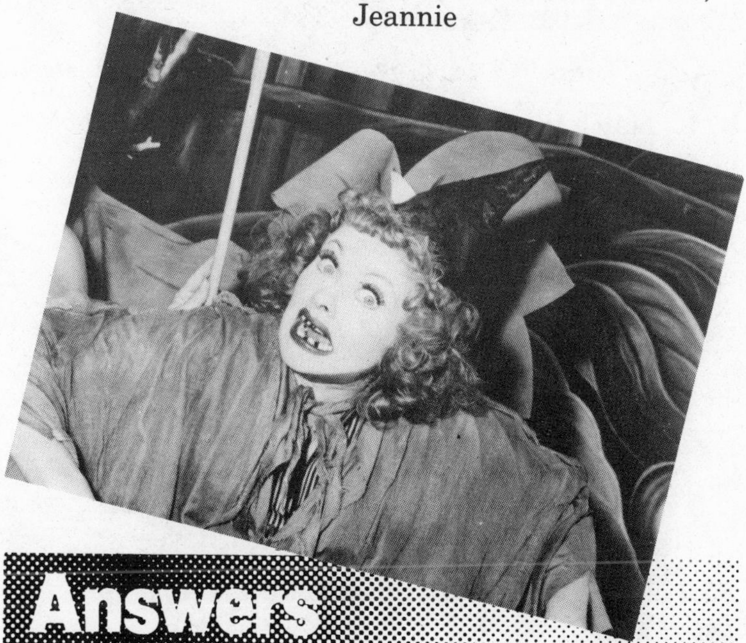

Answers

856. Lucille Ball
857. Kate Jackson
858. Linda Evans
859. Susan St. James
860. Penny Marshall
861. Meredith Baxter Birney
862. Eve Arden
863. Nancy Walker
864. Shelley Fabares
865. Elinor Donahue
866. Connie Sellecca
867. Sharon Gless
868. Stefanie Powers
869. Ann Sothern
870. Barbara Eden

Tough Ones

Questions

Award yourself 2 trivia points for each correct answer.

871. Match the segment of *The NBC Mystery Movie* to its star:

a.	*Amy Prentiss*	Peter Falk
b.	*Hec Ramsey*	George Peppard
c.	*McCloud*	James Farentino
d.	*Columbo*	Rock Hudson
e.	*McMillan and Wife*	Dan Dailey
f.	*Banacek*	Richard Widmark
g.	*Tenafly*	James McEachin
h.	*Madigan*	Richard Boone
i.	*The Snoop Sisters*	Jessica Walter
j.	*Faraday and Company*	Dennis Weaver
k.	*Cool Million*	Helen Hayes

872. What was the first name of the wife in *McMillan and Wife*?

873. What weekly series had a star who always told his lackeys, "Smiles, everyone! Smiles"?

874. What do Jane Jetson and Blondie have in common?

875. What was the name of the Hollywood feature film that premiered *Saturday Night at the Movies* on September 23, 1961?

a. *Casablanca*
b. *Gentlemen Prefer Blondes*
c. *How to Marry a Millionaire*
d. *Some Like It Hot*
e. *The Bridge on the River Kwai*

Answers

871. (a) Jessica Walter; (b) Richard Boone; (c) Dennis Weaver; (d) Peter Falk; (e) Rock Hudson; (f) George Peppard; (g) James McEachin; (h) Richard Widmark; (i) Helen Hayes; (j) Dan Dailey; (k) James Farentino
872. Sally
873. *Fantasy Island* (Ricardo Montalban)
874. Penny Singleton played Blondie and was also the voice of Jane Jetson.
875. (c) *How to Marry a Millionaire*

Trekkie Trivia

Questions

Each Star Trek *question is worth 1 point.*

876. What was the serial number of the U.S.S. *Enterprise*?

877. What was one of Captain Kirk's favorite statements?
- a. "Book em', Dano!"
- b. "One of these days, Alice. POW! To the moon!"
- c. "10-4!"
- d. "Beam me up, Scotty!"
- e. "That's one small step for man, one giant leap for mankind!"

878. Whom did the crew of the *Enterprise* work for?
- a. United Federation of Planets
- b. United Dairy Farmers
- c. Galactic Federation
- d. Universal Peace Patrol
- e. Masters of the Universe

879. Who outranked whom—Mr. Sulu or Ensign Chekov?

880. The creator of *Star Trek* was:
- a. Gene Coon
- b. Eugene Rodney
- c. Gene Roddenberry
- d. Rod Serling
- e. George Lucas

Match the first name to the last name:

881.	Christine	Kirk
882.	Montgomery	McCoy
883.	Janice	Scott
884.	James	Rand
885.	Leonard	Chapel

Answers

876. NCC-1701
877. (d) "Beam me up, Scotty!"
878. (a) United Federation of Planets
879. Mr. Sulu outranked Ensign Chekov
880. (c) Gene Roddenberry
881. Chapel
882. Scott
883. Rand
884. Kirk
885. McCoy

Trivial Songs

Questions

Match the TV show to the singer or group that sang its theme for 2 points each:

886. *Have Gun, Will Travel*	Irene Cara
887. *Secret Agent*	The Ken Darby Singers
888. *The Beverly Hillbillies*	John Sebastian
889. *Fame*	Johnny Tillotson
890. *The Life and Legend of Wyatt Earp*	Frankie Laine
891. *Welcome Back, Kotter*	Sonny Curtis
892. *Karen*	Johnny Rivers
893. *Gidget*	Johnny Western
894. *The Mary Tyler Moore Show*	The Beach Boys
895. *Rawhide*	Flatt and Scruggs

Answers

886. Johnny Western
887. Johnny Rivers
888. Flatt and Scruggs
889. Irene Cara
890. The Ken Darby Singers
891. John Sebastian
892. The Beach Boys
893. Johnny Tillotson
894. Sonny Curtis
895. Frankie Laine

Here's Another Clue for You All!

Questions

Complete these IDs correctly after Clue A for 5 points, after Clue B for 3 points, or after Clue C for 1 point.

896. A. I starred as a doctor on a prime-time TV series.
B. Rachel Ward had the hots for me in *The Thorn Birds*.
C. I was Anjin-san, the shipwrecked navigator, in the blockbuster miniseries *Shogun*.
My name is ______________________.

897. A. I was born in North Dakota.
B. In 1958 I hosted *The Dodge Dancing Party*.
C. With my friends Myron Floren and da lovely Lennon Sisters, I could make champagne music if only I could count past uh-one and uh-two.
I am ______________________.

898. A. I played Jackie Kennedy in a made-for-TV movie.
B. I was Sally Fairfax, a warm, personal friend of the Father of Our Country, in the miniseries *George Washington*.

C. I am best known as an angel—in *Charlie's Angels*—by the name of Kelly Garrett.
My name is ________________________.

899. A. From 1954 through 1962, I was the host of *General Electric Theater*.
B. I replaced Stanley Andrews as the host of *Death Valley Days* in 1965.
C. My best role came in 1981 when I replaced Jimmy Carter as the host of the *Presidential Press Conferences*.
My name is ________________________.

900. A. I was a regular on the short-lived variety series *Van Dyke and Company*.
B. I challenged women to wrestling contests, impersonated Elvis, and lip-synched the *Mighty Mouse* theme song during frequent appearances on *Saturday Night Live*.
C. Though I had a highly publicized fracas with wrestler Jerry Lawlor on *Late Night with David Letterman*, I was best known as Latka on *Taxi*.
My name was ________________________.

Answers

896. Richard Chamberlain
897. Lawrence Welk
898. Jaclyn Smith
899. Ronald Reagan
900. Andy Kaufman

Drive You Crazy

Questions

Rev up your engines for a quiz about the many ways TV leaves the driving (and sailing and flying) to us. Score 1 point for every correct answer.

901. In *The Dukes of Hazzard*, cousins Luke and Bo Duke drive a souped-up Dodge Charger. What is the car's name?

a. Stonewall Jackson
b. General Grant
c. General Lee
d. General Mills
e. Supercar

902. *The Love Boat* rides the waves for ABC. What is the name of the cruise ship?

a. *Atlantic Queen*
b. *Pacific Princess*
c. *Indian Duchess*
d. *Arctic Floozie*
e. *Tallahassee Lassie*

903. What does Richard Simmons' license plate read?

904. What was the name of the atomic submarine in *Voyage to the Bottom of the Sea*?

905. What was the name of the ship in *Battlestar Galactica*?

906. *The Whirlybirds* followed the exploits of a pair of helicopter pilots. Who were they?

a. Pete and Jim
b. P. T. and Chuck
c. Roy and John
d. Bert and Ernie
e. Orville and Wilbur

907. What kind of car is Kitt on *Knight Rider*?

908. In *My Mother, the Car*, Ann Sothern was reincarnated as what make of car?

a. 1919 Stutz Bearcat
b. 1928 Porter
c. 1936 Hupmobile
d. 1941 Studebaker
e. 1958 Edsel

909. Back in the early 1960s, what kind of car helped Tod and Buzz cruise to adventure on *Route 66*?

910. The super race car in *Hardcastle and McCormick* is known as:

a. Coyote
b. Werewolf
c. Roadrunner
d. Palomino
e. Hyena

Answers

901. (c) General Lee
902. (b) *Pacific Princess*
903. YRU FAT
904. The *Seaview*
905. *Galactica*
906. (b) P. T. and Chuck
907. Pontiac Firebird
908. (b) 1928 Porter
909. Corvette
910. (a) Coyote

Fizzies

Questions

Match the star to the TV show that fizzled fast for him. Award yourself 1 trivia point for each correct answer.

911.	Jerry Van Dyke	*Khan*
912.	Clint Walker	*The Family Holvak*
913.	Robert Forster	*Lotsa Luck*
914.	Joe Sirola	*Mr. T and Tina*
915.	Sonny Bono	*Holmes and Yoyo*
916.	Dom DeLuise	*The Montefuscos*
917.	Pat Morita	*My Mother, the Car*
918.	John Shuck	*Nakia*
919.	Glenn Ford	*Kodiak*
920.	Khigh Dhiegh	*The Sonny Comedy Revue*

Answers

911. *My Mother, the Car*
912. *Kodiak*
913. *Nakia*
914. *The Montefuscos*
915. *The Sonny Comedy Revue*
916. *Lotsa Luck*
917. *Mr. T and Tina*
918. *Holmes and Yoyo*
919. *The Family Holvak*
920. *Khan*

Amos 'n' Andy

Questions

In the 1930s, Amos 'n' Andy *was the biggest phenomenon on radio, with many movie theaters emptying out when the show was broadcast. In 1951,* Amos 'n' Andy *became the first TV series with an all-black cast. It was also one of the funniest shows on the air. Score 1 point for each correct answer.*

921. The Kingfish was the real star of *Amos 'n' Andy.* What was the real name of the Kingfish?

922. Who played the Kingfish?

923. What did Amos do for a living?

924. What was the name of the cab company on *Amos 'n' Andy*?

925. Where did *Amos 'n' Andy* take place?

926. Which of the following was Andy's longtime girlfriend?

a. Sapphire
b. Miss Blue
c. Beulah
d. Madame Queen
e. Aunt Esther

927. Amanda Randolph played the Kingfish's mother-in-law, with whom he was always at odds. She later joined another series, playing the same role from 1953 to 1964. What was the role and the show?

928. What were Amos' and Andy's last names?

929. When the Kingfish tried to pull a fast one on Andy, he often used the service of a rather disreputable (not to mention disbarred) lawyer. Who was this barrister?

930. What was the name of the Kingfish's lodge?

Answers

921. George Stevens
922. Tim Moore
923. He was a cab driver
924. The Fresh Air Cab Company of America
925. Harlem in New York City
926. (d) Madame Queen
927. Louise the maid on *The Danny Thomas Show*
928. Amos Jones and Andy Hogg Brown
929. Algonquin J. Calhoun
930. The Mystic Knights of the Sea

First in War, First in Peace, First on the TV Screen

Questions

You can be Number One with us if you answer all these questions about famous firsts on TV. To help you win first place we'll give you 3 points for each correct answer, but first . . . this.

931. Who was the first regular weeknight anchorwoman on the network news?

932. On what show did the Beatles first appear on American TV?

a. *American Bandstand*
b. *The Ed Sullivan Show*
c. *The Jack Paar Program*
d. *Shindig*
e. *The Smothers Brothers Comedy Hour*

933. On what network show did Elvis Presley first appear on nationwide TV?

a. *The Ed Sullivan Show*
b. *The Steve Allen Show*
c. *The Milton Berle Show*
d. *The Jackie Gleason Show*
e. Tommy and Jimmy Dorsey's *Stage Show*

934. What event did NBC televise to inaugurate regular TV service?

a. The signing of the peace treaty with Japan ending World War II
b. The inauguration of Dwight D. Eisenhower
c. The opening of the 1939 New York World's Fair
d. The 1927 World Series
e. Dick Clark's first appearance on *American Bandstand*

935. *Hour Glass*, the first hour-long entertainment series produced for network TV, created TV's first star way back in 1946. This star was:

a. Milton Berle
b. Sid Caesar
c. Ed Sullivan
d. Helen Parrish
e. Jon Gnagy

936. Dick Van Dyke became a TV legend as comedy writer Rob Petrie on *The Dick Van Dyke Show*. But someone else portrayed Rob Petrie in the pilot, shown on July 19, 1960, on *The Comedy Spot*. Who was he?

937. When was the first World Series broadcast on network TV?

938. What was the first regularly scheduled dramatic series on network TV, way back in 1947?

a. *Dragnet*
b. *Treasury Men in Action*

c. *Studio One*
d. *Kraft Television Theater*
e. *The Velveeta Cheese Hour*

939. True or False. The first blacks to have starring roles on network TV series were Bill Cosby in *I Spy* in 1965 and Diahann Carroll in *Julia* in 1968.

940. The Miss America Pageant has been a fixture in Atlantic City since 1921. When was it first telecast on network TV?

Answers

931. Barbara Walters teamed with Harry Reasoner on ABC in 1976.

932. (c) The Beatles appeared on film on *The Jack Paar Program* in January 1964, two weeks before they appeared live on *The Ed Sullivan Show.*

933. (e) Elvis made his first TV appearance on January 28, 1956, on the Dorsey brothers' *Stage Show.*

934. (c) The opening of the 1939 New York World's Fair.

935. (d) Believe it or not, Helen Parris, a child star of the 1930s and hostess of *Hour Glass*, was TV's big star in 1946, at least in the three cities of the NBC TV network—New York, Philadelphia, and Schenectady.

936. Carl Reiner, who later played Alan Brady on *The Dick Van Dyke Show.*

937. NBC telecast the 1947 World Series between the New York Yankees and the Brooklyn Dodgers.

938. (d) *Kraft Television Theater*, which ran from 1947 through 1958.

939. False. *Beulah* starred Ethel Waters and Louise Beavers from 1950 to 1953 and *Amos 'n' Andy*, with an all-black cast, was on CBS from 1951 to 1953.

940. In 1954, with future actress Lee Meriwether winning the crown.

Aunts & Uncles

Questions

We'll give you the names of well-known aunts and uncles on TV series over the years. Name the series they appeared on for 2 trivia points each.

941. Aunt Bea ____________________
942. Uncle Tanoose ____________________
943. Aunt Clara ____________________
944. Aunt Martha ____________________
945. Uncle Charlie ____________________
946. Uncle Fester ____________________
947. Aunt Esther ____________________
948. Uncle Jed ____________________
949. Aunt Harriet ____________________
950. Uncle Bentley ____________________
951. Uncle Bill ____________________
952. Uncle Joey ____________________
953. Aunt Blabby ____________________
954. Uncle Joe ____________________
955. Uncle Martin ____________________

Answers

941. *The Andy Griffith Show*
942. *The Danny Thomas Show/Make Room for Daddy*
943. *Bewitched*
944. *Leave It to Beaver*
945. *My Three Sons*
946. *The Addams Family*
947. *Sanford and Son*
948. *The Beverly Hillbillies*
949. *Batman*
950. *Bachelor Father*
951. *Family Affair*
952. *Circus Boy*
953. *The Tonight Show*
954. *Petticoat Junction*
955. *My Favorite Martian*

Athletes' Feats

Questions

The play is the thing not only for the actor but for the athlete as well. Sometimes the sports star will also make it as a TV star. We'll give you the TV show and the sports team. For 1 point each, you name the athlete-turned-actor.

956. *The Rifleman*—Brooklyn Dodgers
957. *Webster*—Detroit Lions
958. *Chips*—Olympic decathlon medalist
959. *General Hospital*—St. Louis Browns
960. *Hill Street Blues*—UCLA basketball
961. *Hill Street Blues*—Cornell football
962. *The Waverly Wonders*—New York Jets
963. *Ball Four*—New York Yankees
964. *Blue Thunder*—Chicago Bears
965. *Soap*—Olympic pole vaulter

BONUS FOR 3 TRIVIA POINTS Name the professional wrestling manager who has appeared in Cyndi Lauper's rock videos "Girls Just Want to Have Fun," "Time After Time," "She Bop," and "The Goonies 'R' Good Enough."

Answers

956. Chuck Connors
957. Alex Karras
958. Bruce Jenner
959. John Beredino
960. Michael Warren
961. Ed Marinaro
962. Joe Namath
963. Jim Bouton
964. Dick Butkus
965. Bob Seagren

BONUS Captain Lou Albano

Late Night Trivia

Questions

Give yourself 1 trivia point and a shot of caffeine if you can stay awake and answer each of these late night TV questions.

966. When *The Tomorrow Show* became *Tomorrow—Coast to Coast*, who became Tom Snyder's co-anchor?

967. With whom did Paul Schaefer gain fame as a late night bandleader?

968. What do *Saturday Night Live* and the original TV quiz show *Jeopardy* have in common?

969. What network tried a late night programming blitz called *Wide World of Entertainment?*

970. Which of these stars never had his own late night talk show?

a. Joey Bishop
b. Dick Cavett
c. Steven Allen
d. Howard Cosell
e. Jack Paar

971. Ed McMahon is to Johnny Carson as ________ was to Joey Bishop.

972. . . . and as ________ was to Merv Griffin.

973. . . . and as ________ was to Jack Paar.

974. On *Thicke of the Night*, what was Thicke's first name?

975. True or False. Larry "Bud" Melman is the real name of a real person who really appears on *Late Night with David Letterman*.

Answers

966. Rona Barrett
967. David Letterman
968. Announcer Don Pardo
969. ABC
970. (d) Howard Cosell
971. Regis Philbin
972. Arthur Treacher
973. Hugh Downs
974. Alan
975. False. Larry "Bud" Melman is his stage name; his real name is Calvert DeForest.

Trivia Busters

Questions

Answer each of these expert's questions correctly for 2 trivia points.

976. Who was captured live on television as he challenged Senator Joseph McCarthy with the piercing question, "Have you no sense of decency, sir? At long last, have you no sense of decency?"

977. How many Nixon–Kennedy debates were televised?

978. What documentary about refugees from East Berlin was temporarily kept off the air by the U.S. State Department?

979. Charles Collingwood accompanied Jackie Kennedy on a TV tour of the White House in 1962. The tour was broadcast by:

a. ABC
b. CBS
c. NBC
d. All of the above
e. None of the above

980. What TV show took Edward R. Murrow and America into the homes of celebrities?

981. Who sponsored *The G.E. College Bowl*?

982. Who told the world that "our guest is salaried and deals in a service"?

983. Who really killed Richard Kimble's wife in *The Fugitive*?

984. On what comic book was the series *Lost in Space* based?

985. On which of the following shows did the star *not* have a pet chimp?

a. *Sheena, Queen of the Jungle*
b. *Ramar of the Jungle*
c. *Jungle Jim*
d. *Tarzan*
e. They all had a pet chimp

986. "I'm Gonna Sit Right Down and Write Myself a Letter" Department. Mr. T stars as B. A. Barracas on *The A-Team*. What does B. A. stand for?

987. On every episode of *The A-Team*, Mr. T is deathly afraid of:

a. Women
b. Guns
c. Flying
d. Rocky
e. Bullwinkle

988. NBC had a hit miniseries that was brought back in 1984 as a regular series—*V*. What does *V* stand for?

989. Here's the quote, you name the miniseries: "Which one of you bitches is my mother?"

990. Even though some critics complained of too much wind and not enough war, *The Winds of War* was one of the highest-rated miniseries of all time. For 1 point each, name the actor or actress who played:

a. Pug Henry
b. Natalie Jastrow
c. Rhoda Henry
d. Byron Henry
e. Madeline Henry
f. Aaron Jastrow
g. Pamela Tudsbury
h. Franklin Delano Roosevelt

991. Who portrayed the Reverend Jim Jones in the CBS miniseries *Guyana Tragedy*?

992. One of the most powerful miniseries ever shown was *Holocaust*. Which of the following actors won Emmy awards in 1978 for their performances in *Holocaust*?

a. Michael Moriarty
b. James Woods
c. David Warner
d. Meryl Streep
e. Blanche Baker

993. What was the name of *The Wackiest Ship in the Army*?

994. True or False. Vic Morrow starred as Lieutenant Hanley in the TV series *Combat*.

995. What was the name of the detective agency in *77 Sunset Strip*?

996. Cricket was found on:

a. *Tallahassee 7000*
b. *Surfside Six*
c. *Hawaiian Eye*
d. *Hawaiian Heat*
e. *Adventures in Paradise*

997. Who led three lives?

998. Name the five actors who have played Ellery Queen on TV.

999. What was the name of the Menotti Christmas opera that was created especially for television?

1000. What famous actresses/singers were teamed up in a TV special at Carnegie Hall?

Answers

976. Joseph Welch
977. Four
978. *The Tunnel*
979. (d) All of the above
980. *Person to Person*
981. General Electric, of course!
982. John Daly on *What's My Line?*
983. Johnson, the one-armed man
984. "Space Family Robinson"
985. (b) *Ramar of the Jungle*
986. "Bad Attitude" (what else?)
987. (c) Flying
988. Visitors
989. *Lace*
990. (a) Robert Mitchum, (b) Ali MacGraw, (c) Polly Bergen, (d) Jan-Michael Vincent, (e) Lisa Eilbacher, (f) John Houseman, (g) Victoria Tennent, (h) Ralph Bellamy
991. Powers Booth
992. (a) Michael Moriarty, (d) Meryl Streep, (e) Blanche Baker
993. *The Kiwi*
994. False. Vic Morrow starred as Sergeant Saunders. Rich Jason was Lieutenant Hanley.
995. Bailey and Spencer
996. (c) *Hawaiian Eye*
997. Herbert Philbrick (played by Richard Carlson) in *I Led Three Lives.*
998. Lee Bowman, Hugh Marlowe, George Nader, Lee Philips, and Jim Hutton
999. *Amahl and the Night Visitors*
1000. Julie Andrews and Carol Burnett

Sign-Off!

Question

As we reach that point of the book just between Sermonette *and "The Star-Spangled Banner," we want to leave you with the one TV trivia question that has puzzled people all the way back to the days of Milton Berle, Sid Caesar, and Snooky Lanson.*

1001. You know that your TV set can receive Channels 2 through 13 on VHF and Channels 14 through 83 on UHF. *FOR 25 TRIVIA POINTS* Whatever happened to Channel 1?

Answer

1001. In 1948, the Federal Communications Commission (FCC) reassigned the original TV Channel 1 (44–50 megacycles) from broadcast television to nongovernment fixed and mobile services, such as CB radio and radio-called taxis. Since the FCC had already assigned TV channels to stations by 1948, it would have been too difficult, confusing, and impractical to renumber the rest of the TV channels. Therefore, since 1948, there has been no TV Channel 1.

Your Neilsen Trivia Ratings

A total of 1,357 TV trivia points was possible in this book. If you answered every question correctly, pick up the telephone, Call for Glory, *and book an appearance on* Ripley's Believe It or Not!

RATING 40.2/SHARE 61

If you scored 1,158 to 1,356, you could begin a *Dynasty* as a member of *The A-Team* of TV trivia.

RATING 31.7/SHARE 42

If you scored 959 to 1,157, you deserve *Cheers* and will receive *Fame* as a master of TV trivia.

RATING 24.8/SHARE 33

If you scored 760 to 958, *Gimme a Break!* You'll get to keep your *Silver Spoons*, but your TV trivia address has been changed from *Fantasy Island* to *Gilligan's Island.*

RATING 16.9/SHARE 24

If you scored 561 to 759, it is *Not Necessarily the News* that you had better improve on your TV trivia or you'll be singing the *Hill Street Blues.*

RATING 8.3/SHARE 13

If you scored 361 to 560, you are *The Fall Guy* of TV trivia and have been nominated into the Hall of Fame for *Foul-Ups, Bleeps, and Blunders.*

RATING 0.0/SHARE 01

If you scored under 360, you are hereby cancelled!